BEYOND MINDFULNESS
IN PLAIN ENGLISH

Publisher's Acknowledgment

The publisher gratefully acknowledges the generous help of the Hershey Family Foundation in sponsoring the publication of this book.

BEYOND
MINDFULNESS
IN PLAIN ENGLISH

AN INTRODUCTORY GUIDE
TO DEEPER STATES OF
MEDITATION

Bhante Gunaratana

Wisdom

Wisdom Publications
199 Elm Street
Somerville MA 02144 USA
wisdomexperience.org

Library of Congress Cataloging-in-Publication Data
Gunaratana, Henepola, 1927–
 Beyond mindfulness in plain English: an introductory guide to the jhanas / by Bhante Henepola Gunaratana.
     p. cm.
 Includes bibliographical references and index.
 ISBN 0-86171-529-2 (pbk. : alk. paper)
 1. Meditation—Buddhism. I. Title.
 BQ5612.G85 2009
 294.3'4435—dc22
                                        2009009950

ISBN 978-0-86171-529-9   ebook ISBN 978-0-86171-995-2

23 22
8 7 6

Cover design by Gopa&Ted2, Inc. Set in Fairfield LH Light 11 pt. /16 pt.

Wisdom Publications' books are printed on acid-free paper and meet the guidelines for permanence and durability of the Committee on Production Guidelines for Book Longevity of the Council on Library Resources.

Printed in the United States of America.

Please visit fscus.org.

Contents

Preface

$\mathcal{M}$any teachers brought insight meditation, *vipassana*, to the West in the 1970s, and it proved to become very popular. A part of vipassana is the "mindfulness" practice that has come to such prominence today. In the 1980s, many students wanted to read a clear introduction to the practice, but most of the books they could find tended to be scholarly and not very accessible to laypeople. And thus, I wrote *Mindfulness in Plain English*, a how-to book on mindfulness technique and its underlying principles. That book, like this one, was written for ordinary people in straightforward language.

While the words *mindfulness* and even *vipassana* have grown increasingly common and the practice itself has received lots of attention, deep concentration meditation, *samatha*, seems to have received less. In fact, it was widely considered a kind of meditators' Olympics, a pursuit suited only to extraordinary beings who lived in caves or monasteries, far beyond the ken of "normal people," folks with busy daily lives.

In the first decade of this century, interest seems to be turning toward the concentration path. And that is a good thing, because it is truly a parallel yet complementary path to insight meditation, to mindfulness. The two are intertwined and support one another. Over the last two millennia, these two path were codified and refined as parallel paths for a very good reason: they both work, and they work best together. In fact, the two are really one. In truth, the Buddha did not teach samatha and vipassana as separate systems. The Buddha gave us one meditation path, one set of tools for becoming free from suffering.

This book is intended to serve as a clearly comprehensible meditators' handbook, laying out the path of concentration meditation in a fashion as close to step-by-step as possible. Also, this book assumes you have read *Mindfulness In Plain English* or something similar, that you have begun to cultivate a mindfulness practice, and that you are now ready to take the next step—beyond mindfulness.

One note about the structure of this book: throughout it (and especially where talking in detail about the jhanas), I have offered a number of quotations from the canon of Pali suttas, our best record of what it is the Buddha himself taught. Since this is not an academic work, we have not used endnotes. Nonetheless, I'd like to acknowledge the many fine translators whose work I've drawn on in this volume: Bhikkhu Bodhi, Nyanaponika Maha Thera, Bhikkhu Nanamoli, John D. Ireland, and Gil Fronsdal. Additional there are a few translations which are my own, and several that come from the *Visuddhimagga* by Buddhaghosa, translated by Bhikkhu Nanamoli.

And one final note: one of the essential parts of any study is the meaning of the basic terms. There is an extensive and detailed glossary of terms at the back of the book. Please make use of this glossary as you read. Indeed, you can get a very fine review of the material in this book just by reading the glossary.

I am profoundly grateful to John Peddicord for the generous gifts of his time and patience. This book, like *Mindfulness in Plain English*, could not have come into being without his extensive hard work in its development.

I am also thankful to Josh Bartok of Wisdom Publications for making many valuable suggestions to complete the work. Others who contributed their time and effort include Barry Boyce, Brenda Rosen, Fran Oropeza, Bhante Rahula, Bhante Buddharakita, and Bikkhuni Sobhana. I am grateful to all of you.

Bhante Henepola Gunaratana

CHAPTER 1

The Concentration Path

How Much Faith Do You Need?

Though Buddhism is quite different from most religions, and is in some ways more akin to a kind of practical philosophy, the practices and teachings we will be exploring do come from a religious context, namely from Theravadan Buddhism. All you need to do is render the hindrances dormant. All religion depends on some kind of faith, which at heart is nothing more than the willingness to accept provisionally something without yet having proved or verified it for oneself. And this is true with this material as well. But you don't have to be a Buddhist, in any religious sense whatsoever, to gain absorption concentration. Anybody can do it.

So, how much faith do you need? Do you need to convert to Buddhism? Do you need to abandon the tradition in which you were raised or the ideals to which you have deep commitment? Do you need to cast aside anything that your intellect or understanding of the world tells you is true?

Absolutely not. You can retain your current frame of reference and accept only what you are prepared to accept, a piece at time, and only what you in fact find helpful. Yet you do need *some* faith.

You need the same kind of faith that you need to read a good novel or conduct a scientific experiment. You need "a willing suspension of disbelief." I invite you to, as an experiment, put any automatic rejection you may have on hold long enough to see if this path works for you, to see if you yourself can verify what generations of people just like you have verified for millennia.

That temporary suspension of disbelief is all you need here—but even that is not easy. Our conditioned preconceptions are deep and often unconscious. We frequently find ourselves rejecting something without really inspecting that judgment, without even knowing that we have made a judgment. And indeed, this is one of the beauties of the concentration path that we'll be exploring together. It trains us to look at our own minds, to know when we are judging and simply reacting. Then we can decide how much of that instantaneous reaction we wish to accept. You are completely in control of that process.

There is, of course, a snag. You need to be able to suspend your disbelief deeply enough and long enough to give concentration meditation a real, honest, best-effort try, and the deep results are not instantaneous. Do not expect that you can give this a half-hearted effort and two weeks later the heavens will open and the golden sunbeam of inspiration will pour down upon your head. This will almost certainly lead to disappointment.

We are dealing with the deepest forces in the mind, and epiphany is seldom immediate.

Why Deep Concentration Is Important

There is no concentration without wisdom, no wisdom without concentration. One who has both concentration and wisdom is close to peace and emancipation.

The wisdom referred to in this passage is of two varieties. First, there is ordinary wisdom, the kind that can be expressed in words, the kind we know with our ordinary minds. Then there is the wisdom of knowing things at the deepest level, a knowing beyond words and concepts. This book presents you with wisdom of the first kind so that you can seek and find the higher wisdom on your own.

To seek this deep understanding we must quest into the basic nature of the mind itself. In the following passage from the Pali scriptures, the Buddha speaks to his primary disciples and explains the nature of the mind, what makes it ill, and what we have to do to correct that.

> This mind, O monks, is luminous, but it is corrupted by adventitious defilements. The uninstructed worldling does not understand this as it really is. Therefore, for him, there is no mental development.
>
> This mind, O monks, is luminous, but it is free from adventitious defilements. The instructed noble disciple understands this as it really is. Therefore, for him, there is mental development.

In this passage, *"This mind"* is mentioned twice, once for the "uninstructed worldling" and once for the "instructed noble disciple." Yet whether we are ordinary people or advanced meditators, we all have the same kind of mind. The deep mind is constant and luminous, but its light is not light as we ordinarily understand it. The mind, by its very nature, is not dark, murky, or turbulent. In its essential character, it has light; it is bright, filled with a shining, open, non-conceptual intelligence and a deep tranquility.

But all of us have something that keeps it from shining properly. A few of us succeed in removing what is referred to above as "adventitious defilements"— obscurations not inherent to the mind's true nature—and gain "mental development." In the sutta above, "mental development" refers to the deep concentration described in this book. Buddha says that the mind is luminous, but that uninstructed people do not know this. They do not know it, in short, because they do not practice concentration, and they do not practice concentration because they do not know that there is a pure and luminous mind to be experienced.

To achieve concentration we must remove something, and the class of things we must remove are called "defilements." A "defilement" is a corruption, an adulteration, or a contaminant. It is something that muddies the mind. But it is also like a kind of mental toxin. It makes the mind sick. It gives rise to much suffering. But fortunately, these defilements are "adventitious," added from the outside, not part of the deep mind's basic structure.

So: these "adventitious defilements" are qualities of mind we must remove. To attain the benefits of mental development, we must learn what they are and how to get rid of them. This removal operates by cultivating mindfulness and leads to seeing the "luminous" character of the mind.

Sounds interesting, right?

It is.

Sounds like something good to do, right?

It is.

But it is tricky. There are lots of pitfalls along the way and there is plenty to know. But you're holding the right book!

FOLLOWING THE BUDDHA'S EXAMPLE

After his enlightenment, the Buddha went to Banares and delivered his first discourse to a group of disciples known as the Five Ascetics.

These men knew him well. Indeed, they had been practicing self-mortification with him for six long years—until the Buddha realized the shortcoming of the ascetic path and set out toward the Middle Way. As he approached the Five Ascetics, they did not pay him any special respect. They simply called him "friend," just as they had when he was one of them. They did not think he was anybody special. They did not know that he had attained enlightenment.

The Buddha told them of his attainments and that they might now learn from him; he told them outright that he had, in fact, attained enlightenment. They did not believe him. Seeing their skepticism, the Buddha asked them a question:

> "Bhikkhus, have I ever said to you before that I had attained enlightenment?" "No, sir." "So long bhikkhus, as my knowledge and vision of these Four Noble Truths, as they really are, in their three phases and twelve aspects, was not thoroughly purified, I did not claim to have awakened to the unsurpassed perfect enlightenment."

The Buddha was forthright. He knew who he was and what had happened to him. *The Four Noble Truths* are the cornerstone of all his teaching. Each is understood and practiced in three phases. That constitutes what are called the twelve aspects. The three phases are theory, practice, and realization. You must first understand something as a *theory*. Then you put it into *practice* so that you actually experience it taking place. Then you *realize*, that is to say "make real," the result. That is the process by which one verifies a theory as reality. In this usage, the word *realization* means both "understanding" and "final attainment."

The Buddha employed this three-phase method when he uncovered the Four Noble Truths:

The First Noble Truth is that suffering exists. The Buddha knew that suffering was real before he saw it deeply. That is the theory. Actually experiencing the nature of suffering was the Buddha's practice. From his own meditation practice he came to know that suffering is real life and that it should be understood. The Buddha experienced suffering at all conceivable levels. And he learned how to work to overcome it. Finally, the Buddha's realization became perfected. He knew he could end his suffering—and he did it.

The Second Noble Truth is that suffering has a specific cause. The Buddha understood the causes of suffering, exactly as they are, as a theory. His prior practice had led him to this intellectual understanding, but he had not yet realized it fully, experientially. When he did, the Buddha understood that the cause of suffering can be eliminated by eradicating its causes, by ripping it out by the roots. That was the Buddha's practice. He actually did what he said should be done. He attacked the issue at its fundamental layer by eradicating the underlying causes. When he eliminated the causes of suffering fully, the Buddha gained his freedom. That constituted his realization.

The Third Noble Truth is that suffering actually does cease. In theory, the Buddha knew that there is an end to suffering somewhere. As he put this theory into *practice*, he understood that the end of suffering should be attained. He gained the full result of the cessation of suffering as his realization.

The Fourth Noble Truth is that there is a path that leads to the end of suffering. First the Buddha figured out in theory that the path exists. He figured out the steps he needed to take to gain liberation. He put the theory into practice in his own life. And as a result, he was able to clarify the path to liberation as his realization.

The point here is simple. You need to really understand each point of what you are doing, actually *put each step into practice* and actually personally *see the full results* within your own mind. Nothing less will do the job—the ultimate job, the job of becoming free from suffering. Yet this kind of liberation requires full commitment, much work and much patience, and taking the process all the way to perfect realization.

The Buddha gave us the Dhamma, his teachings, so that we can practice. He himself gained the knowledge from his own practice. He did not just come up with an idea, rush out and tell it to the world when it was still just a theory. He waited until he had it all, the theory, the practice, and the full realization. The Buddha gave us a beautiful plan, just the way an architect draws a plan for a building. And, just as builders must diligently follow an architect's careful plans in order to bring the building into being, we too must follow the Buddha's plan to bring liberation into being.

The Buddha gave us a really good, detailed plan. You need to follow it exactly. Other people propose other plans—from the Buddha's time right down to the twenty-first century—but they may not work; they have not been tested by generation after generation for two thousand years.

The Buddha's plan even includes a guarantee: If you follow the instructions given in these discourses exactly, you can attain full enlightenment in as few as seven days. If you cannot get rid of all your defilements, you will attain at least the third stage of enlightenment within seven years.

It's like an extended warranty. Of course, there are a few extra clauses and requirements in the contract, a few ways you can, regrettably, void the warranty. In order to for warranty to be valid, you must:

- Have faith and place that faith in the Buddha, who is free from illness and afflictions.
- Have adequate health and be able to bear the strain of striving.

- Be honest and sincere. Show yourself as you actually are to the teacher and your companions in the holy life.
- Be energetic in abandoning unhealthy states of mind and behavior and in undertaking healthy states.
- Be unfaltering, launching your effort with firmness and persevering doggedly in cultivating wholesome states of mind.
- Be wise. Possess wisdom regarding the rising and disappearance of all phenomena that is noble and penetrative and leads to the complete destruction of suffering.

This book will give you the theory, piece by piece, for how to do all those things. The practice and the realization are up to you. The Buddha reached this perfection of realization of the Four Noble Truths and attained enlightenment by combining concentration and mindfulness in perfect balance.

You can do the same.

THE JHANA ROADMAP

Traveling along the concentration path takes practice. We begin right here, in the world as we know it through our physical senses and our conceptual thinking. If you envision the concentration path as a roadmap, you could say that we all start in pretty much the same geographical region, but each in a slightly different location. That is because we are different personalities and we have accumulated different proportions of the "defilements" that need to be removed through our efforts. We start by performing slightly different cleansing actions, putting the accent on whatever is holding us back the most. Then as we go, our paths converge. What we are doing becomes more and more similar until we are traveling pretty much the same road.

The beginning of the path lies in identifying and deactivating a class of things called *hindrances*. They are the gross aspects of our negative mental functioning and we can spot them easily. To do this we attain and move through special meditative states called the *jhanas*. I'll introduce these in more detail in the next chapter, but for our purposes here it's sufficient to note that in the higher jhanas we temporarily neutralize a class of things called the *fetters*. These are the more subtle factors in the mind that give rise to the hindrances.

Once we have temporarily removed the roadblocks, concentration becomes strong. Then we point it at certain very fruitful objects and look for the characteristics of those objects that lead to freedom.

This is not really as much of a 1-2-3 operation as it sounds. In fact we are doing many of these steps together. Success in each area permits further development in the other areas.

Way down the road, ever-strengthening concentration drops us suddenly into a new landscape. The world of the senses and thinking recedes and we experience four successive stages of joy, happiness, and ever-more subtle kinds of experience. These are the *material jhana* states. They are still on the map of our ordinary world, but just barely.

After that come four more stages that have almost nothing what-ever to do with the world we know right now, through a mind that has not yet experienced such special meditative states. These are the *immaterial jhanas*. They are pretty much off the map of reality as we experience it now.

After that come states called the *supramundane jhanas*. They are, in an important way, clean off the continent of the familiar.

This is the road we will cover together in coming chapters.

CHAPTER 2

Concentration and the Jhanas

Concentration is a gathering together of all the positive forces of the mind and tightly focusing them into an intense beam. Mastering concentration means learning to aim that beam and keep it directed where we want it. This kind of concentration is strong and energetic, yet gentle, and it does not wander away. Building concentration is primarily a matter of removing certain mental factors that hinder its application. We then learn to point the beam at the right things, the really fruitful things within the mind. When we study these things carefully, they cease to bind us and we become free. Concentration, along with awareness, allows the mind to look at itself, to examine its own workings, to find and dissolve the things that impede its natural flow.

How Do We Get There?

We move toward concentration slowly, primarily by weakening certain bothersome factors in the mind and then putting them "in suspension." These things to be weakened are just little things, really—things like terror and anxiety and rage and greed and shame. Just little habits of the mind that are so deeply embedded we think they are natural, that they belong there, that they are somehow *right*, somehow accurate and appropriate responses to the world.

Even further, we think they *are* us; we believe they are somehow embedded in our basic nature and we *identify* with them.

These kinds of things are the basic ways we live, the only way we know how to perceive the world. And we think we absolutely *need* them to survive in the world, that someone who did not think his way through everything would have to be foolish, that someone who was not driven by emotion would have to be a soulless robot at best, and dead at worst.

But all these obscurations and hindrances are just habits. We can learn about them and learn certain skills that put them to sleep for a while. Then, while the hindrances are sleeping, we wakefully can experience directly the shining, joyous, luminous nature of the basic mind that lies below.

When we have experienced how the mind really is, underneath all the mental junk we carry, we can begin to bring pieces of that luminous calm back into our daily lives. Those pieces allow us to carry further the work of undermining the habits we want to remove. This allows deeper concentration, which allows more bliss to seep into our lives. This in turn allows deeper understanding of the habits, which then weakens them further.

And so it goes. It is an upward spiral into peace and joy and wisdom.

But we have to start *here*, right where we are now.

What Are the Jhanas?

The heart of this book is a guide to the jhanas. The jhanas are states of mental function that can be reached through deep concentration meditation. They are beyond the operation of the ordinary, conceptual mind, the mind with which you are reading this book right now. For most of us, this conceptual functioning is all we have ever known and the only thing we can conceptualize. Right now, it's unlikely we can even imagine what it would be like to be beyond thinking, beyond sensory perception, and beyond our enslavement to emotion. This is because the level of the mind that is trying to do the imagining is made up solely of sensing and thinking and emoting. And that is all we may know. Yet the jhanas lie beyond all that. They are challenging to describe because the only words we know are pinned to these concepts, sense impressions, and emotions that have us mesmerized.

The word *jhana* derives from *jha* (from the Sanskrit *dyai*), meaning to "burn," "suppress," or "absorb." What it means in experience is difficult to express. Generally it is translated into English as "a deeply concentrated meditative state" or "absorptive concentration" or even just "absorption."

Translating *jhana* as "absorption" can be misleading, however. You can be absorbed in anything—paying your taxes, reading a novel, or plotting revenge, just to name a few such things. But that is not jhana. The word "absorption" can also connote that the mind becomes like a rock or a vegetable, without any feeling, awareness, or consciousness. When you are totally absorbed in the subject of your meditation, when you merge with or become one with the subject, you are completely unaware. That too is not jhana, at least not what Buddhism considers "right jhana." In right jhana, you may be unaware of the outside world, but you are completely aware of what is going on within.

Right jhana is a balanced state of mind where numerous wholesome mental factors work together in harmony. In unison, they make the mind calm, relaxed, serene, peaceful, smooth, soft, pliable, bright, and equanimous. In that state of mind, mindfulness, effort, concentration, and understanding are consolidated. All these factors work together as a team.

And since there is no concentration without wisdom, nor wisdom without concentration, jhana plays a very important role in meditation practice.

RIGHT CONCENTRATION AND WRONG CONCENTRATION

Right concentration is awake and aware. Mindfulness and clear comprehension are its hallmarks. The mind may be paying no attention to the exterior world, but it knows exactly what is going on within the state of jhana. It recognizes the wholesome mental factors of jhana, without processing them in words, and it knows what they are and what they mean. Mindfulness is the precursor to right concentration. Jhana comes about through restraint of the hindrances. You must have mindfulness to recognize that a hindrance is present in the mind so that you can overcome it. Mindfulness *before* jhana carries over into mindfulness *within* jhana. In addition to mindfulness, clarity, purity, faith, attention, and equanimity must be present in right concentration.

Wrong concentration is absorption concentration without mindfulness. It is dangerous, because you may become attached to the jhanic state. If you realize that what you are doing is wrong concentration, you should come out of it as quickly as possible. The habit is alluring and deepens easily. It is best not to attain wrong concentration at all.

How do you know your concentration is wrong concentration? One indication is that you lose all feeling. There is still feeling in right jhana. It is subtle, but it is present. You lose all feeling only when you have attained the highest jhana known as the attainment of "cessation of perception and feelings." Until such time you certainly have feelings and perceptions.

There are false states in which it appears that you have attained this level. If, when you sit to meditate, your body becomes relaxed and peaceful, you lose the sensation of your breath, you lose the sensations of your body, you cannot hear anything—you should realize that these are sure signs of heading toward sleepiness, not toward the bright wakefulness of jhana. In a moment you will be snoring away, figuratively if not literally too. If you don't feel anything at all, you are not in right concentration.

You can stay in such incorrect absorptions for quite a long time.

Not only Alarakalama has faith, energy, mindfulness, concentration, and wisdom. I too have faith, energy, mindfulness, concentration, and wisdom.

The Buddha said this to Alarakalama and repeated it to Uddakaramaputta. These two men were his former teachers. They had faith, energy, mindfulness, concentration, and wisdom, but not the right kind.

What is the difference between the right kind and the wrong kind? His teachers' qualities were not based on right understanding. They had a strong faith in their own tradition. They had faith in joining their soul with the creator. They used their effort, mindfulness, concentration, and wisdom toward realizing this goal. These are goals that promote a further sense of self and therefore more clinging and more suffering. Therefore their faith, effort, mindfulness, concentration, and wisdom are considered to be of the wrong type.

Ordinarily, when the mind is not concentrated or gains wrong concentration, the notion of self arises. The Buddha's former teachers got stuck in this problem. And this was the breaking-away point for the Buddha. He had been going from place to place and from teacher to teacher in search of truth. He ended up with Alarakalama and Uddakaramaputta. Both of them taught him to meditate and gain the highest immaterial jhana. Fortunately for all us, he decided for himself that more was possible.

These two highly attained meditation teachers could not proceed beyond the highest level of immaterial jhanic concentration into complete liberation. Their concentration did not have right mindfulness or right understanding. They thought what they saw was an entity, a soul, a self, which they thought was eternal, everlasting, imperishable, immutable, and permanent. Right mindfulness would have shown them the truth of selflessness. Concentration without right mindfulness and right understanding is wrong concentration.

CONCENTRATION AND MINDFULNESS

There is an essential relationship between concentration and mindfulness practice. Mindfulness is the prerequisite and the basis of concentration. Concentration is developed and strengthened through "serenity [and] nonconfusion, and mindful reflection upon them." Stated somewhat simplistically, you develop concentration through mindful reflection within a serene and unconfused state of mind. And what are you mindful of? You are mindful of the state itself, the very fact that it is serene and unconfused. As jhana practice is developed, mindfulness gradually increases.

Mindfulness is used to develop your concentration and it is used within the concentrated states to lead to liberation. The most important results of right concentration are the four mundane jhanas, without which right concentration is not complete. Right effort and right mindfulness join together to allow right concentration to reach completion. It is this kind of right concentration that shows things as they really are.

Once you see things as they really are, you become disenchanted with the world of suffering and with suffering itself. This disillusionment with suffering thins down desire and some amount of dispassion arises. Withdrawn from passion, the mind is liberated from desire. This leads to experiencing the bliss of emancipation. Right concentration and right mindfulness always grow together. One cannot be separated from the other.

Both concentration and mindfulness must work together to see things as they really are. One without the other is not strong enough to break the shell of ignorance and penetrate the truth. You may start with concentration and gain jhana, and then use the concentration to purify insight or mindfulness to see things as they are. Or, you may start with mindfulness, then gain concentration to purify mindfulness, so that you can use this purified mindfulness to see things as they really are.

CLEAR COMPREHENSION

Clear comprehension means remaining fully awake and conscious in the midst of any activity, everything your body is doing, and everything you are perceiving. It is a turned-within monitoring of everything going on in the mind and body. Clear comprehension requires "bare attention" ("bare" in the sense of stripped down or nothing added over top) to assure that you are mindful of the right things and mindful in the right way. It is a quality-control factor that monitors what is being noticed and how the noticing is taking place.

You must direct this full, clear, bare attention especially to four things: *The purpose of concentration:* You do it for liberation through seeing the *anicca* (pronounced "ah-NI-chah"; impermanence), *dukkha* (suffering), and *anatta* (no-fixed-self/selfless nature) of all we experience (we will explore these three "marks of existence" in much more detail in chapter 7). You make mindful effort to grasp the purpose of gaining concentration. You are trying to gain concentration in order to understand things as they really are. You are not doing it for pleasure or mental or psychic power.

The suitability of your concentration practice: Are you carrying out your concentration in the right way, paying attention in a mindful way without greed, hatred, and delusion? Or are you dwelling on unwholesome objects and feeding the hindrances? You make mindful effort to understand that all your preparatory works for gaining concentration should be correct to achieve your goal. Many things are necessary for the practice to succeed and you must make them all work for you.

The domain of concentration: What are you concentrating *on*? The proper domain of your concentration is the four objects given in the "four foundations of mindfulness"—specifically, mindfulness of the body, mindfulness of feelings, mindfulness of consciousness, and mindfulness of mental objects. You will learn more about these points in chapter 10. Your domain in gaining concentration is the particular subject of meditation that you have selected to focus your mind upon until finally the mind gains concentration.

The non-delusion of right concentration as opposed to wrong concentration: Are you actually seeing what is there—impermanence, suffering, and selflessness? Is your attention bright, alert, and penetrating the veils of illusion? Or are you seeing what appear to be solid, enduring things with the potential to make you permanently happy or sad?

In truth, the value of clear comprehension goes beyond just the jhanas, you must bring clear comprehension to everything you do. Eat mindfully with clear comprehension; drink, walk, sit, lie down, and answer the call of nature the same way. Mindfully and with clear comprehension, wear your clothes, work, drive and attend to traffic safety, talk, be silent, write, cook, wash dishes. Do it all completely awake to the doing. Try to know everything going on in the mind and body.

These activities, performed with mindfulness and clear comprehension, prepare your mind to attain jhana. When you are truly ready, you attain it without difficulty.

THE BENEFITS OF JHANA

Some teachers say that the jhanas are unnecessary, perhaps that they are rather like playthings for advanced meditators. It may be technically true that some can attain final release from craving, delusion, and suffering without jhanic meditation, but there are many benefits to achieving the jhanas.

First, there is the incredible peace and joy you experience. That feeling is wonderful in itself, and you also bring some of that back with you into your daily life. The vast calm of the jhanas begins to pervade your daily existence.

Even more important is their encouragement to the rest of your practice. The jhanas taste like liberation, a total freedom from all the mental and emotional woes that plague us. But the jhanas themselves are *not* that total freedom; they are temporary states that eventually end, and when they do then your normal world and the suffering-causing way you relate to it creeps back in. But still, they give you the absolute assurance that more is possible, that *your* mind too holds the seeds of complete freedom; through the jhanas you can be assured experientially that liberation is not just a theory, it is not something that could maybe happen to other people but never happen to *you*. In this way, attaining the jhanas gives you incredible energy and encouragement for your practice.

The jhanas teach you the true, strong concentration that is essential for vipassana, the path of insight meditation. The jhanas, especially the fourth jhana (which we will explore in detail in chapter 12), can be used to see impermanence, suffering, and selflessness. Seeing this true nature of reality is the goal of meditation and the jhanas can be used in the service of that goal.

THE POTENTIAL PITFALLS OF JHANA

It's important to know that there are, in fact, certain "dangers" associated with incorrect practice of the jhanas, and a prudent person should be fully informed of the hazards and take them seriously. Here are the two main dangers:

A practitioner of jhana can get "trapped" in jhanic ecstasy.

A practitioner of jhana can build pride around the attainment.

These must be taken seriously. The ego can pervert and co-opt *anything*—even the Buddha's path to liberation—to its own selfish purposes.

Ecstasy is the prime goal of many non-Buddhist contemplative systems. You concentrate on something—an image, a scripture, a sacred stone—and you flow into it. The barrier between self and other dissolves and you become one with your object of contemplation. The result is ecstasy. Then the meditation ends and you are back to the same old you, in your same old life, and same old struggles. That hurts. So you do it again. And again. And again and again and again.

Buddhist meditation is aimed at a goal beyond that—a piercing into the truth of your own existence that dispels the illusion and gives you total, permanent freedom. It is a bit like a railroad track. There is a well-defined track that leads to full emancipation. Incorrect jhana, jhana without mindfulness, can lure you off the track and into a dead-end cul-de-sac. The challenge comes from the fact that this cul-de-sac is in a very attractive location. You can sit there forever enjoying the view. After all, what could possibly be better than profound ecstasy? The answer, of course, is a lasting liberation that frees you from all suffering, not just for the brief period you are maintaining your ecstatic state.

The second danger is also perilous. The jhana states are rare accomplishments. When we attain them we begin to conceptualize ourselves as very special people. "Ah, look how well I am doing! I am becoming a really advanced meditator. Those other people cannot do this. I am *special*. I am Becoming Enlightened!" Some of this may, in fact, be true to a greater or lesser degree. You *are* special. And you *are* becoming an advanced meditator. You are also falling into an ego trap that will stall your progress and create discouragement for everyone around you.

You must take these cautions seriously! The ego is subtle and clever. You can fall into these traps without knowing you are doing so. You can engage in these harmful ways of being with the full conviction that you are *not* doing so!

This is where the teacher enters the picture, someone who has walked the full path her- or himself, and can shepherd the process and keep you from fooling yourself too badly. The value of a true teacher, especially in the middle and later stages of jhana practice, cannot be overstated.

Do please seek one out.

CHAPTER 3

Getting Ready for Jhana Meditation

The Pali literature mentions certain preliminaries for meditation—though in an important way they should not be considered preliminary at all. For most of us this will be our fulltime occupation for quite some time to come.

Our ability to concentrate is hindered at present because our minds are filled with distractions. They are so common and so constant that we think this condition is normal, that it is the way we really are. We think that it is just "the human condition" and that nothing can be done about it. Yet, although it is the current condition of most human minds, it can be changed. A great number of marvelous minds have done it, and they have laid out a series of principles and steps by which we can do it too.

You cannot attain jhana without peace of mind. You cannot have peace without a calm and settled life. You must pave the way with decent behavior and a certain degree of non-involvement in the hectic and alluring things all around you. In this chapter, we'll explore the way to live the kind of settled life that can be a foundation for jhana practice.

MORALITY

The first preliminary is practicing morality. This is the most steady and durable foundation for Buddhist spiritual practice. But Buddhist morality does not mean following rules blindly; there are not a series of *Thou Shalt Nots*. Even so with understanding and determination, you must follow moral and ethical principles. Determination alone does not produce jhana—although you absolutely do need determination to remove obstacles while preparing for the attainment of jhana.

You must apply a *fourfold effort* to get rid of unwholesome habitual practices that hamper your attainment of jhana: With unremitting mindful effort, you try to prevent the formation of any harmful habits that are not currently present. You make the same kind of effort to overcome the unhealthy, harmful habits you already have. You cultivate new, beneficial, wholesome habits that you don't yet have. With the same firm determination, you maintain these new positive habits and perfect them.

Gradually, you build momentum with wholesome thoughts, words, and deeds. When you are mindful and really make an effort to build this momentum, the mind turns naturally toward peace. You find yourself looking for a suitable place and time to develop jhana. You seek out the right posture, subject, and environment.

When you begin the jhana meditation practice, you avoid anything not conducive to gaining concentration. On the cushion, you avoid the hindrances, the reactions that would pull you away from your meditation subject. Off the cushion, you practice the same skills by avoiding the thoughts, words, and deeds that perpetuate the hindrances.

The simplest and most basic moral practice for laypeople is the five precepts. You have to enact two sides of each precept.

One side is to abstain from: killing; taking anything that is not freely given; engaging in any misconduct with regard to sense plea-sures; speaking falsely; taking intoxicants.

The other side is to practice the seven forms of virtuous conduct: friendliness; compassion; generosity; truthfulness; appreciative joy (taking joy in others' good fortune and good qualities); maintaining a sober state of mind; equanimity.

You must apply energy to beginning your program, continuing it and never giving up. You cannot attain jhana without a sense of peace and contentment with your life as it is. Striving to make your life radically other than it actually and presently is will interfere with steady movement toward jhana. Such striving is a form of living for the imagined future; jhana grows out of living in the now. You have to find your present conditions suitable and sufficient or you will always be yearning. You must be content with your food, clothing, and lodging. You need to find contentment in all the situations that arise in your life.

Meditators find from their own experience that, when they prac-tice meditation following moral and ethical principles, their greed, hatred, and delusion slowly diminish. As your meditation makes prog-ress, you see the advantage of morality. Seeing this result, you do not become proud and praise yourself or disparage others. With a humble and impartial mind, you simply recognize that a clean mind—with mindfulness, friendliness, appreciative joy, and equanimity—does make progress in gaining concentration more easily than a mind that is unclean, impure, biased, unsteady, and disturbed.

CONTENTMENT

Contentment means not becoming too greedy for food, clothing, shelter, medicine, or anything else beyond all your other basic req-uisites. The life of one who is content is very easy. The practice of meditation also becomes easy. This Dhamma practice, the practice of jhanas, is for one who is content, not one who is fundamentally discontent.

Practicing mindfulness with clear comprehension makes the mind fully engaged in all the activities you do. You practice mindfulness and clear comprehension while walking forward, backward, looking around, standing, sitting, wearing clothes, and any other mental and physical activities. Everything is included—every action, every thought. Then there is no room in the mind to think of acquiring any material thing or situation. The mind withdraws from the very thought of obtaining something. This is contentment. You need nothing more than the moment provides.

Contentment is being satisfied with wholesome thoughts, words, and deeds. You are content with your friends, relatives, and family members. You are content with your food and eat moderately. You are content with your clothes. You acquire them and wear them moderately. You do everything moderately without being greedy, hateful, or confused. One who is full of contentment feels full all the time. One who is discontented feels something is missing all the time.

One day Mahapajapati Gotami, the Buddha's stepmother, asked him to give her some very brief instruction on Dhamma. One of the things he taught was to cultivate contentment:

> Contentment is the highest wealth. What use is there for a well if there is water everywhere? When craving's root is severed, what should one go about seeking?

RESTRAINING THE SENSES

Observing moral and ethical principles is essential for the successful practice of jhana. This includes restraining the senses.

You should restrain your senses and avoid unwholesome food, unwholesome speech, and unwholesome activities. Restraint of the senses does not mean shutting your eyes when visual objects are present in front of you, or plugging your ears when you hear something. It does not require pinching your nose when there is something to smell. You can still taste your food and touch physical objects.

If shutting off the senses to prevent perceiving any sensory object made a mind clean and pure, then the blind and deaf would have clean and pure minds all the time! Unfortunately, this is not so. We are all human.

In this context, restraint means that, when sensory objects present themselves to your senses, you should focus in a certain way. As a diligent meditator, when you meet a person, do not focus the mind with distorted perception on the general signs of gender, or on the detailed signs of color, height, eyes, ears, nose, lips, hair, legs, or hands. Do not use the mind to enhance or fasten on the person's movements, the sound of the voice, the way the person speaks, looks, or walks.

There are beautiful things all around, beautiful visual objects, sweet sounds, sweet smells, delicious tastes, delightful touches, and compelling thoughts. They are the objects of craving. Our six senses are like hungry animals. They always look for something outside us to consume.

So what do you do instead? You pay mindful attention to your own body and simply mentally note the arising of sense contact. The existence of objects in the world does not cause craving to arise in your mind until you encounter them and reflect on them in an unwise manner.

Craving is one of the most powerful of the unwholesome forces of the mind. It is nourished by the injudicious consideration of these objects. The principal cause of suffering is craving. Once craving is eliminated, much suffering will be eliminated. Still more suffering will be eliminated once ignorance is eliminated. Both craving and ignorance are equally powerful defilements that cause suffering.

In the famous teaching called the "Fire Sermon," the Buddha likens craving to fire. All our senses are on fire, burning with the flames of craving. When one starts meditation, one begins by overcoming covetousness and disappointment. There is a difference between covetousness and greed or desire. With greed and desire, we want things for ourselves. In covetousness, if others have something, we think we should have it.

We begin the practice by overcoming this envious craving and our disappointment in what the world gives us. Here "the world" means our *internal* world. We watch the mind attempting to glue onto something or hold on to something, and we keep that in mindful reflection until it fades away.

SECLUSION

A suitable place for the practice of jhana meditation is strongly recommended. Since we cannot find a place without any noise at all we should find a place with very little noise, with very little sound, and by and large with an absence of human beings, suitable to hide away from human beings and conducive for the practice of solitude.

For jhana practice—for the periods of time you set aside to really do this work—it is very important to leave behind all work, all people, all meetings, all working on new construction or repairing old buildings, all office work, and all family concerns. In other words, all your normal worries and unease. This is physical separation and it is essential. And this the value of a retreat, of physical seclusion.

You need mental seclusion too. Don't carry all your mental baggage with you on retreat. Don't bring your work, your office, mental games, business plans, internal wars and fights with you when you go away. Say goodbye to all of them for a while. Tell them, kindly but firmly, "Don't trouble me now. I will take care of you later on. I know you will be there when I come back."

Another form of seclusion separation is called *liberation from attachment*. This is a real luxury. Gone to a solitary place, you must also separate from the very habit of grasping and clinging. Only then is jhana attainment possible. This kind of mental seclusion is pretty difficult to achieve but absolutely necessary to attain jhana. However, the benefits are enormous. When you don't put energy into thinking about the things that seem so very important, they do gradually disappear from your mind. On the other hand, whatever you often do with your mind, whatever you think about frequently and mentally grab on to, stays in the mind, coming back again and again.

In order to give your mind a little rest, you need to "forget" things deliberately from time to time. This is like draining all the energy from your batteries in order to fully recharge them. When you drain all the energy from the battery of your electronic device and recharge it, the battery lasts longer. Give some rest to your mind. Cease to think about all those duties and responsibilities for a little while. Give the mind full rest by not thinking about anything. When you practice jhana, the mind becomes fresh, clean, pure, and strong. Then you can use that mind to practice vipassana even better. And to take care of your life even more skillfully.

You don't have to go to a cave to attain seclusion. You can do it in a group if all the group members agree to create the physical atmosphere that promotes the state. This is exactly what we do when we attend a retreat. But you don't even need to do that.

You might, for instance, set up a place and time where you can be alone, silent, and undisturbed for at least one hour, a place that is like your own private cave or retreat center. Maybe it is just a closet or a corner of your bedroom. It does not need to be fancy or ornate. It just needs to be somewhere special, withdrawn from the world. It is someplace that you reserve for meditation only, someplace where you can drop everything you are carrying and just do your practice.

A little altar with a statue of the Buddha and some candles is very common, though, of course, not essential. A little bell to start and end your sessions is nice. It can be ornate or starkly simple. Use whatever really reminds you of your own dedication to the practice.

Be prepared to sit solidly for at least an hour. Even if pain arises, try not to move.

Somebody who is really serious in the practice of jhana meditation should make an effort to practice every single day, several times a day. You cannot gain jhana while driving (nor should you try!), or while working in your office, attending meetings, or attending a dinner party. You need a quiet time and a quiet place with reasonably comfortable sitting. The only thing that produces that degree of comfort is consistent, frequent practice.

Mindful Reflection

Before the mind is purified, there are unwholesome tendencies underlying the mind; therefore, greed, hatred, or delusion can arise. You see a form, hear a sound, smell a smell, taste food or drink, and there is an emotional reaction deep in the mind. You touch a tangible object, and there is a reaction. When you even think of some previously conceived image of one of these objects, craving, hatred, or delusion usually arise.

These sensory objects are neither beautiful nor ugly in their own nature. They are simply neutral sensory objects. But when you perceive something with the notion that it is pleasant, yearning arises. If you perceive something with the notion that it is ugly, resentment arises. If your mind is deluded by something's presence, delusion dominates the mind.

Suppose you wear colored glasses and look at objects. You see them according to the color of the lenses you are wearing. If you wear blue lenses, for instance, you see objects as blue. Instead simply look at each arising phenomenon with no lenses at all. Just be mindful of the fact that you have just seen an impermanent object, that you heard a voice, smelled a scent, or saw the movement of a person. Having completed this mindful awareness of the sensory object, you return to your subject of meditation. You should be mindful of what is seen purely as something seen, and what is heard only as something heard. You must simply note anything smelled purely as an instance of smelling, something tasted only as a pure tasting sensation. Something touched is experienced as just a touching. Thoughts and concepts are perceived as just mental objects perceived.

See objects, hear sounds, smell smells, taste food and drink, touch tangible things, and think thoughts *mindfully*, with mindful reflection. Mindful reflection means reflecting on something without greed, hatred, and delusion. It means relating to your environment without notions of "I," "me," and "mine." It means thinking about what is happening without thoughts like, "I am this way or that way," "I love or hate or care nothing about this or that."

When seeing an object, mindfully reflect that it arises depending on a particular sense and a particular object. When the eye, for instance, meets the object you are looking at, there is contact. Then there is a split-second of pure wordless recognition and a particular type of consciousness arises. Depending on the combination of these three—senses, consciousness, and contact—other things arise: feeling, perception, deciding, and thinking.

Then come concepts, labeling, feeling, thought, craving, and detailed thinking. Then comes deliberation or perhaps more elaborate thinking. All of this arises spontaneously and in progression. Most of it is without any conscious will on your part. But all of these are impermanent, unsatisfactory, and selfless. Because they are impermanent, they have already vanished before you blink your eyes, before you can take a single inhalation or exhalation.

Seeing these things is called mindful reflection. When your concentration becomes pure, sharp, clear, and steady, it can penetrate all these veils of distortion and show you things as they really are.

Then the mind opens to penetrate reality more deeply.

Practicing the Noble Eightfold Path

Undisciplined meditators find it very difficult to gain concentration. Discipline, or *shila*, both physical and mental, is absolutely necessary. All those who have attained jhana have practiced shila. There are two sets of disciplinary rules of conduct. One is for the monastic community and the other is for the lay community. The monastic rules are relatively difficult for laypeople to practice. For this reason the Buddha has recommended a stepped-down version for them. It is outlined in the Noble Eightfold Path.

The Noble Eightfold Path constitutes the backbone of how we need to train ourselves in order to attain liberation. The eight steps create the container within which meditation can do its job. The eight steps can be divided into three overarching categories—moral conduct, right concentration, and wisdom. Jhana is included in the concentration group. The eight steps of the Noble Eightfold Path must all be in place in your life in order to create the peaceful, settled atmosphere you need to cultivate jhana.

RIGHT VIEW. Jhana must be pursued and practiced within the context of an overall understanding of what the Buddhist path is all about. Without that view, use of jhana can foster the purposes of ego, rather than eroding them. All use of jhana must be liberation-oriented and supported by mindfulness.

RIGHT RESOLVE. If you do not have firm and clear intentions of what you should be doing and why, you will accomplish nothing or get the wrong result. Three types of right resolve are considered essential. They are the intentions *toward* renunciation (letting go) and *away from* ill will and harm.

RIGHT SPEECH. You need to set up habits of speech conducive to your practice. Speaking is important. Every word you say colors your mind. Things like lying and frittering away your time talking about trifles will not help you at all. And moreover, speech can reinforce habits of mind: speaking coarsely and unkindly, for instance, actually strengthens the hindrances of anger and aversion.

RIGHT ACTION. What we do comes back to us. What we put out into the world creates the emotional environment in which we live. Robbing a bank is clearly not conducive to the depth of calm and tranquility necessary to achieve jhana. Even eating your neighbor's apple agitates the mind. Tiny misdeeds accumulate to create enough tension in the mind to keep you from the goal.

RIGHT LIVELIHOOD. Making your living as a thief or a drug dealer obviously does not promote peace, but those are only gross examples. Even small, dubious business practices disturb the mind. Does your job harm someone or something, even indirectly? You either carry the tension and guilt of your deeds or you deaden yourself to them. Neither will allow you to achieve jhana. Bringing care and consideration to the means by which you make your livelihood is essential.

RIGHT EFFORT. Obtaining jhana is not easy. We have to make certain efforts to create the conditions that allow it to manifest. We must honestly generate an aspiration to achieve it or it won't happen. Then we have to actually try. Then, once we have it, we have to foster it, preserve it, and maintain it. This is a matter of genuine intention and doing some real work.

RIGHT MINDFULNESS. Mindfulness cannot become strong without concentration. Concentration cannot become strong without mindfulness. To achieve jhana we keep the hindrances dormant. It is mindfulness that notices the nature of the content of each moment of hindrance so that we can surmount it.

RIGHT CONCENTRATION. Right concentration is using the mind in the direction of jhana. You don't need to succeed at that in order to make progress on the Path, but the benefits of doing so are considerable.

Anyone who is interested in practicing meditation to attain jhana should, without exception, practice these ethical principles.

But don't wait until your morality is perfect to start the practice for attaining jhana. When you meditate with imperfect morality, soon you will realize that it is very difficult to attain concentration. One hindrance or another gets in your way. Then you make mindful effort to understand and overcome that hindrance. You repeat this trial and error method and one day you will attain jhana. Yet it takes time and patience and the willingness to simply start again each time you slip.

MINDFULNESS

Mindfulness, as we have seen, is your first and most important tool for starting to build the foundation of jhana and jhana itself. You must make a mindful effort to understand unwholesome things as unwholesome and wholesome things as wholesome. You must make a mindful effort to overcome the unwholesome and to cultivate every wholesome thought, word, and deed that you can. When you practice jhana, you must make mindful effort to understand what you are doing, to prepare the mind to attain jhana.

All of us from time to time encounter people who "push our buttons." Without mindfulness, we respond automatically with anger or resentment. With mindfulness, we can watch how our mind responds to certain words and actions. Just as you do on the cushion, you can watch the arising of attachment and aversion. Mindfulness is like a safety net that cushions you against unwholesome action. Mindfulness gives you time. Time gives you choices. Choices, skillfully made, lead to freedom. You don't have to be swept away by your feeling. You can respond with wisdom and kindness rather than habit and reactivity.

When you engage in your activities mindfully, you realize for yourself that certain thoughts, like greed, hatred, and confusion, trouble your mind and you don't gain even a little concentration, let alone jhanic concentration. Then, from your own experience, you come to know, "Well, I need a break from all these negative thoughts." At that point you deliberately begin to cultivate wholesome and positive thoughts.

Since greed and ignorance work as a team to generate suffering, you cannot eliminate suffering without eliminating both greed and ignorance. The Buddha pointed out how the practice of meditation can bring an end to your suffering and allow you to experience the bliss of peace.

If you respond to insults or angry words with mindfulness, you can look closely at the whole situation. Perhaps the person who harmed you was not paying mindful attention to what he or she was saying. Perhaps he or she did not mean to hurt you. The person might have said what he or she said totally innocently or inadvertently. Perhaps you were not in the right mood at the time the words were spoken. Perhaps you did not hear the words clearly or you misunderstood the context.

It is also important to really consider carefully what that person is saying. If you respond with anger, you will not hear the message behind the words. Perhaps that person was pointing out something you needed to hear. Actually listen to what the person is saying and do not get angry while doing so. Anger opens your mouth and seals your ears.

Development of mindfulness helps us relate to others with loving-friendliness. On the cushion, you watch your mind as liking and disliking arise. You teach yourself to relax your mind when such thoughts arise. You learn to see attachment and aversion as momentary states and you learn to let them go. Meditation helps you look at the world in a new light and gives you a way out of anger. The deeper you go in your practice, the more skills you develop. The ultimate use for mindfulness is seeing impermanence in action. Everything else is a stepping-stone toward that goal.

Mindfulness is always present in right jhana or indeed in any wholesome activity. So, all the way along the Path, you should endeavor to do everything with mindfulness. Then it becomes a habit. It becomes simply the way the mind functions most of the time. That way, when you attain jhana, mindfulness will be present in your jhana.

THE FIVE SPIRITUAL FACULTIES

The five spiritual faculties are *mindfulness, wisdom, energy, faith*, and *concentration*. In truth, you cannot practice right concentration by itself in the absence of the other faculties.

When you try to gain *concentration*, hindrances arise. In order to overcome hindrances you must use *mindfulness*. Whatever method you employ to overcome hindrances must be employed with mindfulness to make it work. One such method, the cultivation of loving-friendliness, is explored in the next chapter.

The *energy* factor is needed too. It boosts your practice. When you practice mindfulness and concentration, they work well only if you have adequate energy. Without energy you will be sluggish and lazy. You will not be able to make much progress.

Faith, as we have seen, is also an important factor. You will not have any initiative to practice if you don't have faith in the Buddha, Dhamma, and Sangha. In this context this means trusting that someone (the Buddha) has indeed attained what you yourself are trying to attain, that there exists a roadmap (the Dhamma) that will help you attain it, and that there are people (the Sangha) who can guide you and accompany you on the path to liberation.

Wisdom comes into play too. You must be wise enough to really understand why you are launching yourself on this path. What are your real goals? Which ones do you really believe in and which are just something you read in a book or heard from someone else?

All the five spiritual faculties must work together in order for you to proceed smoothly with the practice.

People sometimes ask me to tell them more about what I mean by this word "wisdom." Here is one answer that I give.

As you keep paying total undivided attention to everything you experience in your body, feelings, perceptions, volitional formations, and consciousness, all you can honestly see with your mental eye is that everything is constantly changing. Certain things you experience are pleasant; certain things are unpleasant; and certain things are neither-pleasant-nor-unpleasant. But all of them, without any exception, are constantly changing.

Your ordinary state of mind is not aware of these changes. So, in spite of their changes, your mind, even without your awareness, does three things: clings to the pleasant; rejects the unpleasant; and gets sucked into the neither-pleasant-nor-unpleasant.

This last is especially important. This neither-pleasant-nor-unpleasant business is tricky. It is ordinary, everyday experience. It is so familiar that you think this neither-pleasant-nor-unpleasant state is the experience of your soul or permanent self, the "real me."

This clinging to the pleasant, rejecting the unpleasant, and confusing the neither-pleasant-nor-unpleasant experiences with "reality" is a naturally built-in system.

This clinging, rejecting, and getting confused changes too. With meditation your intuition tells you that this repetition of changing— arising and passing away of all your experiences, this pleasant, unpleasant, and neither-pleasant-nor-unpleasant—this is not satisfactory, not a happy situation.

Seeing this frustrating situation, your mind gets tired of all experience, even the pleasant ones. Then your mind lets go of clinging to any pleasant experience; it lets go of any unpleasant experience; it lets go of any neither-pleasant-nor-unpleasant experience.

Then you experience peace within yourself. Then your mind becomes free from greed, hate, and delusion. This particular skill, power, or faculty, or the strength of liberating the mind from these three poisons, three weapons, or three kinds of fire is what Buddhists called true wisdom.

Each of the six senses is sometimes called "ocean." Each ocean is full of dangers of sharks, demons, waves of greed, hatred, and delusion. The clear vision of using them skillfully is wisdom. The Buddha summarizes this like this:

One who has crossed this ocean so hard to cross, with its dangers of sharks, demons, waves, the knowledge-master who has lived the holy life, reached the world's end, is called one gone beyond.

CHAPTER 4

Wishing the Best for Yourself and Others

The force of loving-friendliness within the mind is called *metta* in Pali. It means wishing the best for yourself and others. Metta is also used to refer to mental exercises we use to cultivate this loving-friendly state of mind. We say specific words and think specific thoughts in order to generate a pure feeling. Generating metta is one of the principal routes *to* jhana. It is also a specific remedy for states of mind that keep us *from* jhana.

In fact, metta makes the perfect preparation for jhana-oriented meditation. It clears away the hindrances so that concentration may arise.

LOVING-FRIENDLINESS IN THOUGHT AND ACTION

Practicing loving-friendliness meditation can change your habitual negative thought patterns and reinforce your positive ones. When you practice loving-friendliness meditation, your mind will become filled with peace and happiness. You will be relaxed. You will gain concentration.

But loving-friendliness is not limited to your thoughts. You must manifest it in your words and your actions, too. And it involves others, not just yourself. You cannot cultivate loving-friendliness in isolation.

You can start by thinking kind thoughts about everyone you have contact with every day. If you have mindfulness, you can do this every waking minute with everyone you deal with. Whenever you see someone, consider that, like yourself, that person wants happiness and wants to avoid suffering. We are all the same. We all feel that way. All beings feel that way. Even the tiniest insect recoils from harm.

When you recognize that common ground, you see how closely we are all connected. The woman behind the checkout counter, the man who cuts you off you on the expressway, the young couple walking across the street, the old man in the park feeding the birds, and the birds themselves. Whenever you see another being, any being, keep this in mind. Wish that one happiness, peace, and well-being. It is a practice that can change your life and the lives of those around you.

The meditation center where I teach is in the hills of the West Virginia countryside. When we first opened our center, there was a man down the road who was very unfriendly. I encountered him regularly on the long walk I take every day. It is a quiet forest road with little traffic and I always wave at everyone who goes by. Whenever I saw this man, I would wave to him. He would just frown at me and look away. Even so, I would always wave and think kindly of him, sending him loving-friendliness. I was not disappointed by his attitude. I never gave up on him. Whenever I saw him, I waved just as I did with other people. After about a year, his behavior changed. He stopped frowning. I felt wonderful. The practice of loving-friendliness was bearing fruit.

After another year, when I passed him on my walk, something miraculous happened. He drove past me and lifted one finger off the steering wheel. Again, I thought, "Oh, this is wonderful. Loving-friendliness is working." Another year passed. Day after day, when I took my walk, I would wave to him and wish him well. The third year, he lifted two fingers in my direction. Then the next year, he lifted *all four fingers* off the wheel. More time passed. One day I was walking down the road as he turned into his driveway. He took his hand off the steering wheel, stuck it out the window, and waved to me.

One day, not long after, I saw him parked on the side of one of the forest roads. He was sitting in the driver's seat smoking a cigarette. I went over to him and started talking. First we chatted just about the weather and then, little by little, his story unfolded. It turns out that he had been in a terrible accident. A tree had fallen on his truck. Almost every bone in his body was broken. He had been in a coma. When I first started seeing him on the road, he was only beginning to recover. He did not refrain from waving because he was a mean person. He did not wave because *he could not move all his fingers.* Had I given up on him I would never have known how good this man is.

To top it all off, one day, when I had been away on a trip, he actually came by our center looking for me. He was worried because he hadn't seen me walking in a while.

Now we are friends.

CULTIVATING FRIENDLINESS TOWARD DIFFERENT TYPES OF PEOPLE

You need to find reasons to develop loving-friendliness toward those you have problems with. A few traditional analogies describing five different types of people may help guide you here.

The first type of person is someone whose deeds are rotten. He does bad things and has a very base manner. He does not know how to behave. He is not polite. His manners are rough. He does not show respect to anybody.

Venerable Sariputta compared such a person to a dirty rag. Suppose a traveling monk sees a dirty rag on the road in front of him. It is so dirty that he cannot even pick it up with his hands. He holds it by one foot and kicks it with the other foot and dusts it off. He cleans it off that way—only with his feet. Then he picks it up with two fingers and shakes it off with contempt. Then he takes it home, washes it neatly, and puts it to some use. He might use it to patch up a robe or make a doormat. He puts that piece of cloth to work.

This metaphor teaches us, when you want to cultivate loving friendship for such a person, you find one reason or another.

The layers of dirt on the rag are like the layers of conditioning on this person that have made him so rough and impolite. Maybe he has acquired this from his parents, his teachers, his associates, his education, and his upbringing. Maybe he has been discriminated against. Maybe he has been mistreated and abused and intimidated in his childhood. Maybe he is not an educated person. All kinds of things you do not know about may be contributing to his rough behavior. These are his history. You do not know about these things, but it is best to forgive him for all his misdeeds. Practice metta toward him.

He is suffering from his own hatred and he deserves our compassion. He does not know how to deal with his own suffering. Perhaps he has lost his friends, his home, his job, his relatives, due to his own hatred. Maybe he has had a terrible divorce. All we can see is that he is suffering. All we can do is practice compassion.

Maybe this helps to reduce his hatred and make him happy, maybe it doesn't. If it doesn't, we practice equanimity toward him. This is a balanced state of mind, but it doesn't mean we just give up. We think of other ways to help him.

You may discover a second kind of person with bad words whose deeds are good. This is someone who has no polite words in his vocabulary, only foul language, yet he or she nonetheless does something good for you or for the world.

This person might see you frustrated at doing things improperly. He may come up to you and say, "You fool! You idiot! You don't know how to do this. You're going to kill yourself if you do it that way. Here, let me do it!" Then maybe he does the whole job for you. That is a good reason for you to develop loving-friendliness toward that person.

This person, in spite of his filthy language, may do something wonderful. For that, you must respect him, admire him, and you share loving-friendliness with him. Help him change his way of talking. When you associate with him and show your loving friendship for him, he will perhaps gradually change. You arouse loving-friendliness within yourself for that person, and that, in turn, can arouse it in him.

This second person is compared to a pond covered with algae. When you want to dive into it or get water out of it, you have to remove the moss by hand, and only then can you dive in and swim properly. Similarly, you learn to ignore such an algae-covered person's superficial weaknesses. You watch and you find out that her heart opens to compassion and loving friendship from time to time. She develops a pure heart from time to time. That is a good reason for you to develop loving-friendliness toward this second person.

A third person may have both bad words *and* bad deeds, yet a flickering impulse toward kindness within. This person is like a puddle on the road. Suppose you are walking on a road where there is no water, no well. You are thirsty and tired. You are hungry and thirsty, desperately looking for some water to drink. You are almost dehydrated. At that time, you find a little water in a cow's footprint. There is not too much water because a cow's footprint is not too deep, but there is a little water in it. If you try to take that water by hand, you make it muddy. So, what do you do? You bend down, kneel down, and slowly bring your mouth close to that bit of water. Then sip it without disturbing the mud. Even though it is dirty and muddy, you may still quench your thirst for a moment. You sip the water gently and leave the mud behind. In this way we can see at least the *potential*, from time to time, for even such a person bad in word and deed to, in certain circumstances, open his heart to noble things, friendly things, and compassionate things. You should practice loving-friendliness toward such a person, in spite of all his weaknesses.

You meet another person, a fourth person. This person's words are bad, his behavior is bad, and his heart does not open at all for anything noble. This person is like a patient, a sick man, walking on a road where there is no hospital, no village, and no humans around, no one to help him. There is no water, no house to rest in, no tree to give shelter, just the hot sun and his burning thirst. This person is afflicted and suffering from a severe sickness. He really needs medical attention; otherwise he will surely die. You see him and you feel very sorry for him. Your heart melts. You think, "How can I help this suffering being? What can I do for him? He needs water, medicine, and clothes. He needs somebody to help him. How can I help him?" In spite of all those difficulties, and despite the fact that you will almost certainly receive no gratitude, you nonetheless resolve to be of service.

When I meet such a person I think thoughts like this, "With bad bodily conduct and bad verbal conduct like this, he is committing many unwholesome and unskillful acts. He is suffering from that now and he will suffer from it in the future. Let me help him get rid of his hatred."

A fifth person's thoughts are sweet and wonderful. His words are beautiful and friendly. His deeds are friendly, beautiful, and pure. Everything is ideal. It is, of course, very easy for us to cultivate loving-friendliness toward that person. Even so, doing this mindfully can be of great value.

You must try to cultivate loving-friendliness equally toward all these five people without discrimination. This is not very easy. You have to make a great sacrifice—a sacrifice of your comfort, a sacrifice of your thoughts, a sacrifice of your feelings and your attitudes. You have to sacrifice many things in order to cultivate loving-friendliness. You must remember that the overall purpose of what you are doing here is to make *yourself* calm and peaceful, to make your mind and body healthy, and to make your surroundings healthy. You are trying to make others feel comfortable in associating with you. To make them comfortable, you first make yourself comfortable with them. When you feel comfortable to associate with others, you carry on your conversations and activities harmoniously. You have to take the initiative to lay the groundwork and prepare yourself to practice loving-friendliness.

When you come to truly understand suffering, your heart opens to the hidden nature of your own loving-friendliness. Then you feel so much love and compassion for all living beings that your mind naturally wishes them all to live in peace and harmony.

Over the years, I have received many letters from prisoners who are seeking to learn the Dhamma. Some have done terrible things, even murder. They see things differently now and want to change their lives. There was one letter that was particularly insightful and deeply touched my heart. In it, the writer described how the other inmates shouted and jeered whenever the guard appeared. The inmate tried to explain to the others that this guard was also a human being. But the others were blinded by hatred. All they could see, he said, was the uniform, not the man inside it. This man was putting loving-friendliness into action and it altered his perceptions.

Loving-friendliness is not something you do by just sitting on a cushion, thinking and thinking and thinking. You must let the power of loving-friendliness shine through your every encounter with others. Loving-friendliness is the underlying principle behind all wholesome thoughts, words, and deeds. With loving-friendliness, you recognize more clearly the needs of others and help them readily. With thoughts of loving-friendliness you appreciate the success of others with warm feeling. You need it in order to live and work with others in harmony. It protects you from the suffering, fear, and insecurity caused by anger and jealousy. When you cultivate your loving-friendliness, your compassion, your appreciative joy for others, and your equanimity, you not only make life more pleasant for those around you, your own life becomes peaceful and happy. The power of metta is like the radiance of the sun, beyond measure.

Loving-friendliness goes beyond all boundaries of religion, culture, geography, language, and nationality. It is a universal and ancient law that binds all of us together—no matter what form we may take. Loving-friendliness should be practiced unconditionally. My enemy's pain is my pain. His anger is my anger. His loving-friendliness is my loving-friendliness. If he is happy, I am happy. If he is peaceful, I am peaceful. If he is healthy, I am healthy. Just as we all share suffering regardless of our differences, we should all share our loving-friendliness with every person everywhere.

No one nation can stand alone without the help and support of other nations, nor can any one person exist in isolation. To survive, you need other living beings, beings that are bound to be different from yourself. That is simply the way things are. Because of the differences we all have, the practice of loving-friendliness is absolutely necessary. It is the common denominator that ties all of us together.

Why Metta Is Important for Jhana

You cannot practice mindfulness without loving-friendliness, nor can you practice loving-friendliness without mindfulness. These two always go hand-in-hand. When you are flowing metta to all living beings, radiating it outward in all directions, with your whole mind, on every sense channel, when you are doing it sincerely, there is simply no room for the hindrances. You cannot radiate good will and be greedy at the same time. You cannot be fearful or angry. You cannot have doubts, restlessness, boredom, or dullness.

When you practice loving-friendliness you build up a very powerful spiritual magnet that pulls people toward you. You feel very comfortable wherever you go. You feel that everybody around you is friendly toward you. You feel secure thinking that everybody around you is friendly. You can trust them. You can leave home knowing that your friends protect your home. You feel comfortable that your friends protect your family.

Your metta practice makes you so relaxed and peaceful that you are pleasing to all around you. You can sleep well. You will not have nightmares. You can get up with a fresh feeling. You can talk to anybody without anger. You like them, and they often like you in response.

The practice of loving-friendliness is also a healing meditation for the one who does it. It heals all the wounds of anger. When the power of loving-friendliness repels anger, you are very relaxed and joyful.

Remember, it is crucial to extend loving-friendliness to yourself as well as to others. Your practice will not succeed if you harbor animosity or indifference toward yourself. Practicing loving-friendliness toward yourself first makes you peaceful and happy. Resting in that experience, you can wish others the same peace and happiness by cultivating loving-friendliness toward them. You send it out from a calm, peaceful, compassionate center and that must start with yourself.

MEDITATIONS ON LOVING-FRIENDLINESS

This section presents six formal meditations on metta. The metta practice has three levels. The first is the verbalizing level, the second is the thinking level, and the third is the feeling level. When you are in jhana, you experience the feeling level of metta.

General Instructions

Start with the words and ideas. Say the formal words given below, or some variant of them. These are just examples provided here to show the progression of beings involved and how to extend your metta outward. You start with yourself as a focal point for peace and good wishes; then expand your area of focus outward by stages until it includes the entire universe of beings.

If the formal words do not resonate with you, you can use words that are truly meaningful to you.

Envision *specific* people or animals in each category. Hold them clearly in mind. Make the feelings real and personal. Some categories and types of people are more challenging than others. Work on each category until you can do it fluidly and sincerely.

Explore the physical feelings associated with metta. Find out, deeply and with mindfulness, exactly what is going on in your body, exactly where it is happening and precisely how it feels.

Focus on the physical feelings until they become a pure distillation of all the thoughts and physical sensations. It is a feeling beyond sensation, almost an emotional coloring in the mind. It is often accompanied by sensations of warmth and swelling in the area of the heart.

Drop the words, the images, the beings, the physical feelings, and the stages. Move deeply into the pure feeling of metta as an intangible thing, beyond simple thought, emotion, and physical feelings. Get the living essence of the thing.

Use yourself as a kind of radiator to pump the pure feeling of friendliness and kindness out to the whole universe. Stay with that.

Metta meditation has the potential to carry you into jhana. The pure feeling of metta as an experience can be used to carry you across the barrier into the wordless. It is very close to the feelings that predominate in the first jhana and it can be used as a tool to reach them.

Metta Meditation 1

May *I* be well, happy, and peaceful. May no harm come to me. May I always meet with spiritual success. May I also have patience, courage, understanding, and determination to meet and overcome inevitable difficulties, problems, and failures in life. May I always rise above them with morality, integrity, forgiveness, compassion, mindfulness, and wisdom.

May *my parents* be well, happy, and peaceful. May no harm come to them. May they always meet with spiritual success. May they also have patience, courage, understanding, and determination to meet and overcome inevitable difficulties, problems, and failures in life. May they always rise above them with morality, integrity, forgiveness, compassion, mindfulness, and wisdom.

May *my teachers* be well, happy, and peaceful. May no harm come to them. May they always meet with spiritual success. May they also have patience, courage, understanding, and determination to meet and overcome inevitable difficulties, problems, and failures in life. May they always rise above them with morality, integrity, forgiveness, compassion, mindfulness, and wisdom.

May *my relatives* be well, happy, and peaceful. May no harm come to them. May they always meet with spiritual success. May they also have patience, courage, understanding, and determination to meet and overcome inevitable difficulties, problems, and failures in life. May they always rise above them with morality, integrity, forgiveness, compassion, mindfulness, and wisdom.

May *my friends* be well, happy, and peaceful. May no harm come to them. May they always meet with spiritual success. May they also have patience, courage, understanding, and determination to meet and overcome inevitable difficulties, problems, and failures in life. May they always rise above them with morality, integrity, forgiveness, compassion, mindfulness, and wisdom.

May *all people to whom I am indifferent* be well, happy, and peaceful. May no harm come to them. May they always meet with spiritual success. May they also have patience, courage, understanding, and determination to meet and overcome inevitable difficulties, problems, and failures in life. May they always rise above them with morality, integrity, forgiveness, compassion, mindfulness, and wisdom.

May all *unfriendly persons* be well, happy, and peaceful. May no harm come to them. May they always meet with spiritual success. May they also have patience, courage, understanding, and determination to meet and overcome inevitable difficulties, problems, and failures in life. May they always rise above them with morality, integrity, forgiveness, compassion, mindfulness, and wisdom.

May *all living beings* be well, happy, and peaceful. May no harm come to them. May they always meet with spiritual success. May they also have patience, courage, understanding, and determination to meet and overcome inevitable difficulties, problems, and failures in life. May they always rise above them with morality, integrity, forgiveness, compassion, mindfulness, and wisdom.

Metta Meditation 2

Having seen that all beings, like yourself, have a desire for happiness, you should methodically develop loving-friendliness toward all beings.

May I be happy, and free from suffering! And, always, like my self, may my friends, neutral persons, and hostile ones be happy too.

May all beings in this town, in this state, in other countries, and in the world systems be ever happy.

May all persons, individuals, beings, and creatures in all world systems be ever happy.

So too, may all women, men, noble ones, non-noble ones, gods, humans, and beings in the lower worlds be happy.

May all beings in every direction and every place be happy.

Metta Meditation 3

May I be free from hatred. May I be free from affliction. May I be free from worry. May I live happily.

As I am, so also may my parents, teachers, preceptors, and friendly, indifferent, and hostile beings be free from hatred. May they be free from affliction! May they be free from worry. May they live happily! May they be released from suffering. May they not be deprived of their fortune, duly acquired.

May all beings... all living things... all creatures... all persons... all those who have arrived at a state of individuality, all women... all men... all noble ones... all non-noble ones... all gods... all humans... all non-humans... all those who are in the hell, and in this home, village, town, this country, in this world, in this galaxy, may all of them without any exception be free from worry. May they live happily. May they be released from suffering. May they not be deprived of their fortune, duly acquired.

Metta Meditation 4

May those with no feet receive my love. May those with two feet receive my love. May those with four feet receive my love. May those with many feet receive my love.

May those with no feet not hurt me. May those with two feet not hurt me. May those with four feet not hurt me. May those with many feet not hurt me.

May all beings, all those with life, be happy.

May suffering not come to anyone.

May those suffering be free from suffering. May the fear-struck be free from fear. May the grieving be free from grief.

So too may all beings be.

From the highest realm of existence to the lowest, may all beings arisen in these realms, with form and without form, with perception and without perception, be released from all suffering and attain to perfect peace.

Metta Meditation 5

May all beings be happy and secure. May all beings have happy minds.

Whatever living beings there may be without exception—weak or strong, long, large, medium, short, subtle, or gross, visible or invisible, living near or far, born or coming to birth—may all beings have happy minds.

Let no one deceive another nor despise anyone anywhere. Neither from anger nor ill will should anyone wish harm to another.

As a mother would risk her own life to protect her only child, even so toward all living beings one should cultivate a boundless heart.

One should cultivate for all the world a heart of boundless loving-friendliness above, below, and all around, unobstructed, without hatred or resentment.

Whether standing, walking, or sitting, lying down or whenever awake, one should develop this mindfulness; this is called divinely dwelling here.

Metta Meditation 6

Let me direct my mind in the eastern direction and wish all living beings in that direction to be free from greed, anger, aversion, hatred, jealousy, and fear. Let these thoughts of loving-friendliness embrace all of them, envelop them. Let every cell, every drop of blood, every atom, every molecule of their entire bodies and minds be charged with these thoughts of friendliness. Let their bodies and minds be relaxed and filled with the peace and tranquility of loving-friendliness. Let the peace and tranquility of loving-friendliness pervade their entire bodies and minds.

Let me direct my mind to the southern direction and wish all living beings in that direction to be free from greed, anger, aversion, hatred, jealousy, and fear. Let these thoughts of loving-friendliness embrace all of them, envelop them. Let every cell, every drop of blood, every atom, every molecule of their entire bodies and minds be charged with these thoughts of friendliness. Let their bodies and minds be filled with the thought of loving-friendliness. Let the peace and tranquility of loving-friendliness pervade their entire bodies and minds.

Let me direct my mind to the western direction and wish all living beings in that direction to be free from greed, anger, aversion, hatred, jealousy, and fear. Let these thoughts of loving-friendliness embrace all of them, envelop them. Let every cell, every drop of blood, every atom, every molecule of their entire bodies and minds be charged with these thoughts of friendliness. Let their bodies and minds be relaxed and filled with the peace and tranquility of loving-friendliness. Let the peace and tranquility of loving-friendliness pervade their entire bodies and minds.

Let me direct my mind to the northern direction and wish all living beings in that direction to be free from greed, anger, aversion, hatred, jealousy, and fear. Let these thoughts of loving-friendliness embrace all of them, envelop them. Let every cell, every drop of blood, every atom, every molecule of their entire bodies and minds be charged with these thoughts of friendliness. Let their bodies and minds be relaxed and filled with the peace and tranquility of loving-friendliness. Let the peace and tranquility of loving-friendliness pervade their entire bodies and minds.

Let me direct my mind to the celestial direction and wish all living beings in that direction to be free from greed, anger, aversion, hatred, jealousy, and fear. Let these thoughts of loving-friendliness embrace all of them, envelop them. Let every cell, every drop of blood, every atom, every molecule of their entire bodies and minds be charged with these thoughts of friendliness. Let their bodies and minds be relaxed and filled with the peace and tranquility of loving-friendliness. Let the peace and tranquility of loving-friendliness pervade their entire bodies and minds.

Let me direct my mind to the animal realm and hell realms and wish all living beings in that direction be free from greed, anger, aversion, hatred, jealousy, and fear. Let these thoughts of loving-friendliness embrace all of them, envelop them. Let every cell, every drop of blood, every atom, every molecule of their entire bodies and minds be charged with these thoughts of friendliness. Let their bodies and minds be relaxed and filled with the peace and tranquility of loving-friendliness. Let the peace and tranquility of loving-friendliness pervade their entire bodies and minds.

May all beings in all directions, all around the universe be beautiful; let them be happy; let them have good fortune; let them have good friends; let them after death be reborn in heavens.

May all beings everywhere be filled with the feeling of loving-friendliness, abundant, exalted, measureless, free from enmity, free from affliction and anxiety. May they live happily.

May all those who are imprisoned legally or illegally, all who are in police custody anywhere in the world waiting trials be met with peace and happiness. May they be free from greed, anger, aversion, hatred, jealousy, and fear. Let these thoughts of loving-friendliness embrace all of them, envelop them. Let every cell, every drop of blood, every atom, every molecule of their entire bodies and minds be charged with these thoughts of friendliness. Let their bodies and minds be relaxed and filled with the peace and tranquility of loving-friendliness. Let the peace and tranquility of loving-friendliness pervade their entire bodies and minds.

May all of them in all directions, all around the universe be beautiful; let them be happy; let them have good fortune; let them have good friends; let them after death be reborn in heavens.

May all children abused by adults in numerous ways be free from pain, afflictions, depression, disappointment, dissatisfaction, anxiety, and fear. Let these thoughts of loving-friendliness embrace all of them, envelop them. Let every cell, every drop of blood, every atom, every molecule of their entire bodies and minds be charged with these thoughts of friendliness. Let their bodies and minds be relaxed and filled with the peace and tranquility of loving-friendliness. Let the peace and tranquility of loving-friendliness pervade their entire bodies and minds.

May all of them in all directions, all around the universe be beautiful; let them be happy; let them have good fortune; let them have good friends; let them after death be reborn in heavens.

May all rulers be gentle, kind, generous, compassionate, considerate, and have best understanding of the oppressed, the underprivileged, the discriminated against, and the poverty-stricken. May their hearts melt at the suffering of the unfortunate citizens. May the oppressed, the underprivileged, the discriminated against, and the poverty-stricken be free from pain, afflictions, depression, free from disappointment, dissatisfaction, anxiety, and fear. Let these thoughts of loving-friendliness embrace all of them, envelop them. Let every cell, every drop of blood, every atom, every molecule of their entire bodies and minds be charged with these thoughts of friendliness. Let their bodies and minds be relaxed and filled with the peace and tranquility of loving-friendliness. Let the peace and tranquility of loving-friendliness pervade their entire bodies and minds.

May all of them in all directions, all around the universe be beautiful; let them be happy; let them have good fortune; let them have good friends; let them after death be reborn in heavens.

CHAPTER 5

Breath Meditation

*I*n addition to the loving-friendliness meditations we have just explored, there is another kind of meditation of inestimable value to building the foundation of jhana practice: breath meditation.

How to do breath meditation is a large topic. It has been thoroughly covered in the first book in this series, *Mindfulness in Plain English*. If you are uncertain of the technique, please see that book or any other well-respected primer on the subject (the recommendations for further reading in this volume offers suggestions). But for our purposes now, I will offer just a brief recap. This section just lays out some simple pointers on applying breath meditation toward the goal of achieving deep concentration.

First, fasten the mind on the breath and hold it there. You may start with the rise and fall of the abdomen and the chest, but then you should switch over to the breath at the nostrils or the upper lip. This is where you will get a single, distinct point of sensation.

Stay with that single point of sensation. When other thoughts, feelings, or perceptions pull you away, notice them just enough to see their impermanence, their fleetingness. They rise, stay a bit, and then fade away. Just see that, over and over. In this way, every distraction from your object of focus acts as a stepping-stone toward your process of liberation. Seeing the impermanence in every distraction—just that, all by itself—may be enough to lead you into genuine concentration.

If distractions refuse to go away or keep coming back, analyze which hindrance is present. Then apply one or more of the remedies presented in the next chapter.

Also bear in mind that sometimes your mind is like a cup of muddy water. How can you get clear water from a cup of muddy water? All you have to do is to set the cup on flat ground. Then the sediment settles down and the clear water stays on top. Similarly, when the mental sediment has settled down, your mind becomes clear. Then you should be able to sit, ideally, for one solid hour. Even if you have aches and pains, you should not move (though don't sit in a position that needlessly causes you excruciating pain). Let the physical sensations move into the background.

When you want to gain concentration, don't go into the details of the breath—rising, falling, and so forth. If you happen to notice the rising and falling of breath, the movement of the abdomen, and so forth, don't worry about it. Just go ahead and notice them until your mind settles down. Do not investigate or elaborate. Stay with the overall feeling of breath as a single, flowing process. Don't think or categorize or conceptualize. Then the mind switches over to pure concentration all by itself.

Vipassana Awareness of the Breath

Sometimes when you begin to meditate, your mind is restless. It's very hard to center on the breath and stay there. You need something interesting to hold your attention. But what could possibly be interesting about the breath? You've had it all your life and you take it for granted. Isn't breath the most boring thing in the world?

There *is* something going on. In fact, there are, by traditional reckoning, *twenty-one* things going on, over and over. They are things you can notice, things you can make the subject of your vipassana awareness. You can notice each of them as a separate event if that helps you keep your attention on the meditation object.

Twenty-one points of repetition occur with every inhaling and exhaling.

Inhaling has: a beginning; a middle; an end; a brief pause.

Exhaling has the same four events. That is eight points.

We can also identify the following four points: *Pressure*—When the lungs are full with inhaled breath we experience pressure; *Release*—There is a release of pressure when we breathe out; *Anxiety or urgency*—When you breathe out and the lungs are empty of breath, there is a small degree of anxiety or urgency; *Relief of anxiety or urgency*—When you breathe in, the anxiety fades away and you experience relief.

The *four elements* are there, too: *Earth element*—The breath touches your nostrils, the tip of your nose or the upper lip, and inside the nose between the eyes. This touch is sometimes hard and sometimes soft. That is an expression of the earth element; *Water element*—Sometimes breath is dry and sometimes moist. This is due to the presence of the water element in the air we breathe in and out; *Heat element*—Sometimes breath is warm and sometimes cool; *Air element*—The air itself is, of course, present in the breath.

You can also observe the *five aggregates*, the traditional constituents of your body and mind. The five aggregates are form, feeling, perceptions, volitional formations, and consciousness: *Aggregate of form*— Breath has a kind of a shape to it. Because of the presence of the four elements in the breath, the ancient texts refer to breath as *a body*: the body of breath; *Aggregate of feeling*—We must feel the breath to notice that it is there for us to use as object of meditation; *Aggregate of perception*—We must mentally perceive the breath in order to identify its presence. This cognitive function belongs to the perception aggregate; *Aggregate of volitional formation*—We intentionally pay attention to our breath, feeling, and perception; *Aggregate of consciousness*—And, last but not least, we cannot do any of them without consciousness.

These twenty-one points are always repeatedly present, and mindful breath meditation can bring them all into awareness.

Notice especially the points about anxiety or urgency, its coming and its going. Anxiety motivates much of our behavior, especially the parts we would be better off without. There is much to be learned here about the function of your own emotional life. Full-blown anxiety often manifests as constant recurring thoughts about your situation, some sensation in the area of the heart, lungs, and stomach, plus an almost undetectable "flavor" in the mind. Here is your chance to study how small anxiety manifests for you so that later, when anxiety is strong, you will be able to study it further. This is an excellent practical application of your vipassana skills.

The Four Elements

The four elements is an analytical system to help you develop mindfulness. It works very well with the practice of mindfulness of breathing meditation. This is an ancient categorization scheme for looking at the nature of our own experience. It analyzes every experience we have in terms of symbolic qualities that are like some of the primary things we see in the normal world: earth, water, air, and fire.

Please keep in mind that these are not mere words, nor are they some highly philosophical or mystical qualities only available to deep thinkers and spiritual supermen. These are things you are experiencing right now. It is just a different way of analyzing the experience you are having at this very moment. Each of the four elements manifests in the single practice of mindfulness of breathing.

The *earth* element represents the property of solidity, heaviness, solidness, compactness. Its characteristics are hardness or softness.

Just feel yourself sitting. Place your attention on that solid feeling where your body touches whatever you are sitting on. Feel your feet pressing against the floor. Those are hard sensations. Feel the light touch of the air against your skin. That is a soft sensation. This is the earth element.

The breath itself shows you the earth element. The breathing can be hard or soft. You would not feel anything unless there were solid flesh doing the feeling and you can feel that solidity. You feel whatever part of the body the air contacts as hard. You feel the solidness of the abdomen as it rises and falls. You feel the solidity of the nostrils as the air passes over them. Sometimes the breath has a roughness to it. Sometimes a gentle breath is so soft you can scarcely feel it.

It's a very simple concept, really. It's so simple that we totally overlook it unless somebody points it out to us.

Mindfulness of breathing shows us the *hard*, *soft*, and *solid* qualities of our experience.

The *water* element has a moist or flowing quality. The blood pumps through your veins. Your stomach pulses and gurgles with digestion. There are various squishing and swishing feelings happening within you right now. And most of the time you ignore them. When you get quiet in meditation they stand revealed. Any sensation that is damp, humid, or clammy in nature is in this category too.

Breath has a flowing quality. Sometimes you feel the moisture as humid air comes in. When the external air is dry, you can feel that it is more moist as it goes out. As you concentrate on the breath, other sensations from the rest of the body intrude. Some of them have this flowing quality too.

Mindfulness of breathing shows us the *liquid*, *moist*, and *flowing* qualities of our experience.

The *air* element is experienced primarily as motion or stillness. The moving quality of anything is the air element expressed through that thing. You experience little tinglings and vibrations in the skin. It feels like something is moving. There may be deep grinding feelings inside that have a moving quality. The flow of blood, the same sensation that revealed the liquid factor, can also show you the air element if you open up to it as pure movement.

The air element can also be experienced as space—the space within which movement of breathing takes place. Sometimes the body feels like an empty house, a vacant space, a mere shell within which all kinds of things are taking place. Maybe nothing is taking place. You still have the element of air present as the feeling of an empty locality within which there is absence or stillness.

The breath is constantly moving. The abdomen fills; it rises and falls. The physical air moves in and out. Even in the pauses there is a feeling of hollowness or vacuum within which it all happens.

Mindfulness of breathing shows us the *moving*, *still*, or *spacious* quality of our experience.

The *fire* element manifests as heat or cold or any sense of temperature in between. It also manifests as the dry sensation that goes with heat. When you feel hot and want to be cooler, the pure feeling that precedes the thought is the fire element manifesting. The temperature in the room drops and you feel cold. That is the fire element manifesting. The temperature feels neutral and you have to really seek to feel any temperature at all. That is the fire element too.

Any sensation within the body that has an energetic or burning or chilling quality is the fire element at work. There are feelings that go *zing* and *zoom*. They vibrate very fast. There are burnings and acidic stingings.

The air often feels cool against the nostrils on the in-breath, warmer on the out-breath. That is the fire element. You become distracted by the temperature around you. You feel the temperature of the physical air against your skin. That is fire manifesting.

Mindfulness of breathing shows us the *hot-cold* or *energetic* quality of our experience.

So… what is the point of this four elements category scheme?

We contemplate the *four elements of the breath body* as a meditation exercise to examine our own experience with precision. With every passing material experience that we see in meditation we silently ask, "Which of the four qualities predominates here?" The whole purpose is to push us, almost against our will, into contact with the pure, experiential essence of sensory reality. Training the mind to see the impingements of material experience as simply elemental vibrations helps to break down our usual mental habits. It frees us from the concepts that usually arise and the mental reactions to those concepts.

And, like all other vipassana meditation, when the intense examination carries you into the wordless, non-conceptual observation of what is happening, you drop the words, drop the labels, and just sit in the midst of change.

Developing a Daily Meditation Practice

The most effective daily regimen I have found is to combine the two primary practices presented here. You use metta meditation to prepare the mind for jhana and then use either the breath or the pure feeling of metta to carry you into the jhana state.

The advantage of using the breath is that it is a habit that most of us have developed and cultivated throughout our meditation career. It is something we already have. For most of us, when the mind is quiet it swings naturally to the breath. We have trained it to do that. The advantage of metta is the similarity between the pure feeling of metta, with its calm and joy, and the feelings that predominate in the jhana state.

Which you choose is a matter partly of your own personality. You use the one that works best for you. But remember to start with metta and, if you are going to switch to the breath, let metta make the mind still. Quite often the mind swings to the breath naturally out of habit. The switch should be gentle, if possible, occurring by itself.

You might begin with a formal recitation of your intentions. You want to really feel it in a personal way. It is often very effective when expressed in your own thoughts, your own private internal language, the way you normally talk to yourself inside your head. I often use something like this:

Let me clear my mind of all resentment, anger, and hatred. Let me banish all want and need and agitation. Let my mind be bright and awake and aware. Let it be filled with friendly feeling.

Let the clear mind experience clear Dhamma. Let my mind be filled with compassion. Let me have metta so that I can feel other people's suffering and my own joy. Let me have strength to practice without difficulties. Let me find peace and joy and give them to everyone.

I want to keep my mind alert throughout this session. I want to attain concentration. I honestly want to understand the Dhamma so that I can share my understanding of Dhamma with everybody. I don't have any ulterior motive. I do it for myself and everybody else. We all benefit.

I want my mind to be clear. I want everyone's mind to be clear. I want to find peace and joy for myself and everyone everywhere.

I am doing this for myself and everybody. I am clearing my mind to taste the peace and joy that lies down at the roots of my mind, down under the thoughts. I want peace and joy for myself and everyone. I want to see impermanence happening before the eye of wisdom so that I can be free and help everybody else become free too.

You may use any words you like to generate the friendly, peaceful thoughts in your mind. Make it real. The formal recitations are a good place to start, but your own thoughts often work better.

Remember your goal: to see the impermanence in all experience. Keep mindfulness bright and clear. Spot every hindrance that arises. Know which hindrance it is and see it when it is present. Use the tools presented in the next chapter to overcome each one. Watch it. Know when it is present and when it is no longer there. See its impermanence.

When the mind becomes quiet and still and joyous, let the attention glide to the breath or ride the pure feelings of peace and contentment and good will into jhana.

Stay with your object of attention. Rest the mind on it. Watch it. Watch for "the sign" to arise. (We will have more to say later about what exactly this means.) Watch yourself watching for it and notice your own desire or any other reaction. Stay with the object. Know peace.

Remember, jhana happens when it happens. It cannot be forced or rushed. Every apparent failure is a step toward success. When it doesn't happen as you want it to, use mindfulness to notice the feelings of frustration that arise. Every time you do that, you are strengthening your mindfulness and moving one step closer to the goal.

You cannot lose unless you give up.

CHAPTER 6

Why Can't We Concentrate
Strongly Right Now?

Why do we have to learn to concentrate? Why do we have to practice to develop a skill that, theoretically, should be a natural, built-in characteristic of the mind? The simple fact of the matter is that we have to do it because distractions arise to pull us off the track. These distractions get in our way and impede our progress along the path.

Our minds are filled with thoughts and emotions that we think are normal. They are powerful and alluring, even in small doses. They suck us right in and dominate our attention. They are distractions. The mind cannot focus in the presence of these disturbances.

Try not to think of a dinosaur.

Just for one minute, sit right there and do not think about a pink dinosaur. Think about a jet aircraft instead. Stop reading and do that right now.

Doesn't work very well, does it? The power of suggestion pulls us back to that pink dinosaur image pretty strongly, doesn't it? And, for most of us, a pink dinosaur is not something with which we are really obsessed. But how about paying the bills when your bank account is empty? How about sex and romance and your job and that guy who hates you? Those things are much more powerful. Have you ever tried to study or meditate after a tough day, when everything has gone wrong and you feel exhausted and confused? Very difficult.

The Pali suttas list five things that are the most powerful distractions for all of us. These hindrances interfere with our concentration, on the cushion or off.

Sensual Desire. We see something and we want it, or we think of something and we want it. We want to be surrounded by good music. We want the room to be cooler or warmer. We want that new car. We want that great dinner. And we want them all right now. Once a thought like that enters the mind, it keeps coming back and back and back until we get what we want or despair of ever getting it. We obsess over it. We think about it night and day. We sacrifice the genuine good things in life for shiny baubles. The thoughts are incessant and obsessive. We cannot keep the mind on anything else for long.

Ill Will (Aversion). We hate being sick. We hate that nasty noise. We hate this food and we want something else. We wish that mean person who gives us such a rough time would go drop in a hole and vanish. Whenever life gives us something we really abhor, our mind gets stuck on it. It destroys our concentration power.

Restlessness and Worry. We don't want to get cancer. It hasn't happened yet and it may never happen, but if it seems even remotely possible, we worry about it. We don't want to lose our job, or get a divorce, or be in a traffic accident. We worry and fret. We scheme how to get things and dwell on the possibility of not getting them. The thoughts keep us up at night and distract us from the good things right in front of us. Sometimes we just can't sit still, and we cannot even say why. Nervous anxiety fills us; the body trembles and the mind flits from one useless thing to another. We absolutely cannot concentrate in this state.

Sloth and Torpor. Sometimes we are just too tired, mentally, physically, or both. Sleepiness feels sweet and we want it. We have just no drive or energy. Sometimes we just can't focus clearly. When we try to read, we read the same paragraph three times and it just does not make sense. When we try to meditate, the mind is like a swirling grey fog; everything is hazy and indistinct. So maybe we give up and go watch TV or something else that will pound its way in through the dullness. Concentration requires energy, vigor, clarity, and sharpness. In this state we just do not have it.

Doubt. Sometimes we start to meditate or do something else and we are full of indecision. We wonder, "Am I really getting anywhere with this? Is it really worth my time? How do I know if any of what I have been told is true? Am I doing it right? Am I doing it wrong?" There is just no certainty. The mind wavers and dithers and shies away from the task. We may put it off until we are totally sure of something or other. But total certainty in life seldom comes and the task never gets done. Sometimes life requires a bit of a gamble and a bit of trust. Without it we just can't keep the mind on one thing.

How the Hindrances Are Nourished

Hindrances appear as a result of three types of erroneous behavior: *wrong thoughts* (thoughts of greed, hatred, and cruelty); *wrong speech* (false speech, malicious speech, harsh speech, and gossip); and *wrong deeds* (killing, stealing, and misconduct in sensual pleasures).

In addition, there are some harmful habits that nourish hindrances: *Unmindful reflections.* Whatever we dwell on embeds emotional responses in our minds. The repeated emotions turn into habits that trap us. We must pay attention to our habitual thoughts and the objects on which our perceptions habitually linger, or we contaminate the minds we are trying to cleanse.

Not listening to true Dhamma. It is not easy to escape from our trap. The route is subtle and easily misunderstood. We must examine the source of the ideas that we think are going to save us. Among other things, we must be sure that the source of the ideas has no hidden agenda. Many things can sound wonderful in words. To determine the worth of any particular system, we must carefully inspect what type of person that system actually produces. Systems that are spread through force, bigotry, or propaganda pressure are probably not going to move us in the direction of peace and wisdom.

Associating with unwholesome friends. We soak up ideas, attitudes, and actions from the people around us. We should seek to associate only with people who are equal to or better than we are.

Concentration and Mindfulness Block Hindrances

Concentration holds the hindrances at bay. Correspondingly, in order to achieve concentration, we must block these hindrances from our minds temporarily by using mindfulness. When we succeed in blocking the five hindrances, we experience a great relief. This relief slowly increases until it becomes joy.

Mindfulness and clear comprehension belong to the realm of the insight practice, but in order to practice jhana we must use mindfulness to overcome the obstacles to our concentration. The hindrances don't disappear automatically. Mindfulness and concentration must work together.

We must use mindfulness to know five things about the hindrances: when they are present; when they are absent; how they arise; how to let them go; how to prevent them from arising in the future.

TECHNIQUES FOR OVERCOMING HINDRANCES

When you are distracted by a hindrance during your meditation practice, take a moment to think about which hindrance is predominating in the mind. Then apply one or more of the methods in the list. We will look at all of these hindrances by looking at their symptoms, their nutriments (those factors that maintain the hindrances), and potential solutions to each one.

Sensual Desire

Symptoms: Distracting thoughts about what you want to get, do, have, or attain. Most of our distracting thoughts have an element of wanting something to be different from the way it is. Planning is always like this. The thoughts are incessant and obsessive. You cannot keep the mind on anything else for long.

Nutriments: Giving frequent, unmindful attention to the thoughts in the desire category. The nourishment of sense desire is unmindful reflection, and the route to overcoming it is mindful reflection.

Solutions: You are dwelling on something. You cancel that by making the mind dwell on healthier things:

• *Pure mindfulness*—When a desire arises, notice that it is present. When it disappears, notice that it is absent.

• *Mindful reflection*—Generate a genuine, healthy desire to rise above this unmindful reflection and get rid of it. Generate its opposite, mindful reflection.

• *Self-encouragement*—You can actually talk silently to yourself, reminding yourself of wholesome intentions.

• *The Noble Eightfold Path*—The most direct way of getting rid of sense desire forever is the cultivation of the entire Noble Eightfold Path. Recall the steps. Which one is lacking at this moment? Which one is most lacking in your life? Resolve to work on that.

Ill Will (Aversion)

Symptoms: When your thoughts reveal a motivation that is unkind or aggressive, even a little, you have ill will. In that condition you cannot appreciate the beauty of anything or anybody. When it reaches the level of grudge or hatred, you are like a pot of boiling water, very hot and confused. The thoughts are incessant and obsessive. You cannot keep your mind on anything else for long.

Nutriments: Dwelling on your angry thoughts. Ill will can start from a mild annoyance or some slight irritation. If you don't take care of it at that level, it gradually grows into aversion, resentment, anger, grudge, or hatred. This comes from unmindful reflection on the subject of your anger. You dwell on it. You contemplate it, think about it again and again. You feed it.

Solutions: Catch anger at the outset—Be mindful of it as soon as it arises. Don't let it build.

• *Isolate anger*—Isolate it in the mind as an event separate from the actions, persons, situations, or memories that trigger it. Let anger just mirror in your mind without being a person who is angry. Let it be just a pure energy.

• *Talk to yourself*—Give yourself a kind but thorough lecture.

• *Count breaths*—Count your breaths in the very special way described below.

• *"Homage to the Blissful One"*—Bring your respect for the Buddha and his teachings into play. Say, "Homage to the Blissful One, the Worthy One, the Fully Enlightened One." Say it three times. Remember the Buddha's infinite patience, compassion, and loving-friendliness.

• *Remember that your temper is dangerous*—and remember anger's miserable consequences.

• *Try to see the whole person*—Stop dwelling only on the negative aspects of the person or situation. Remember the good parts.

• *See impermanence and dependent origination*—Use anger to enhance your overall realization of the truth. See that anger and its causes are impermanent. Realize that anger and its causes are impermanent. See that anger arises dependent on causes and conditions.

• *Be kind to yourself*—Sometimes you are angry with yourself too. Forgive yourself. Recall your good qualities and what you are striving to become.

• *Remember that you will die*—Do you really want to pass away with this in your mind? Remember that, when you do or say something with anger to hurt somebody, you hurt yourself first. You hurt yourself even before you hurt the other.

• *Don't blame anybody*—Remember that it is just a situation. The other person has a viewpoint too and it looks as valid to him or her as yours looks to you.

• *Cultivate gratitude*—Use metta to cultivate gratitude toward everybody. It dissolves anger and ill will.

• *Talk to the pain*—Anger causes pain and pain causes anger. Talking to the pain, talking to your laziness, talking to aging, talking to fear—all these can be very useful and important.

Ill will is a very large topic. It's not just anger that sticks to us. It's things like sadness and fear and depression too. You can have ill will toward anything—the pain in your back or leg, the taste of your dinner, the house you live in or your salary. This section has presented remedies that apply to human relationships—your interactions with the people around you. But the general principles you have read on these pages apply to anything toward which you have aversion. I invite you to think about how you will apply what you have read to the real situations of your life—your illness, paying your taxes, and the death of your dearest friend.

Restlessness and Worry

Symptoms: You have "monkey mind," fear, tension, anxiety, and a nervous, jittery feeling manifest in a mind jumping continually from thought to thought. You just cannot settle down, mentally or physically. Sometimes it is all too subtle and you cannot pin it down. Sometimes it is so strong that you do not have enough focus to see any of it clearly.

Nutriment: Frequently giving careless attention to the thoughts of worry and the feelings of restlessness.

Solution: Count your breaths in the very special way described below.

Sloth and Torpor

Symptoms: Sloth and torpor is the traditional description given to all sleepy, lethargic, sluggish states of mind. *Sleepiness and drowsiness* is another common translation. Sometimes you are just too tired, mentally, physically, or both. Sleepiness feels sweet and you want it. You have just no drive or energy. Sometimes you just can't focus clearly. Concentration requires energy, vigor, clarity, and sharpness. In this state you just do not have it.

Nutriments: When you do mindfulness of breathing, body and mind become relaxed. You often feel sleepy and lethargic. Sleepiness is very sweet. You want to welcome it in, invite it to stay. But real joy does not arise from sleepiness or drowsiness. Don't deceive yourself by identifying the cloying sweetness of sleepiness with real joy. It makes you dull. You lose your energy. The Buddha said: "This Dhamma is for developing energy, not for developing laziness."

Solutions: Try one of the following techniques.

• *Mindful reflection*—In lethargy too, you must apply your cognitive form of mindful reflection. Conduct a silent monologue to rouse yourself, giving yourself encouragement and motivation.

• *Open your eyes*—Open your eyes and roll your eyeballs around for a few seconds. Close them and go back to your sitting mindfulness exercise.

• *Visualize a bright light*—Visualize a very bright light and focus your mind on it for a few seconds. As you are visualizing bright light, the sleepiness often fades away.

• *Hold your breath*—Take a deep breath and hold it as long as you can. Then slowly breathe out. Repeat this several times until your body warms up and perspires. Then return to your sitting practice.

• *Pinch your earlobes*—Pinch your earlobes hard with thumbs and index fingers. Really feel the pinch. Surprisingly, this can help.

• *Standing*—Stand up very slowly and very quietly. Try to do it so that even a person sitting next to you will not know. Do standing meditation for a few minutes until the sleepiness goes away. Once it is gone, return quietly to your sitting mindfulness practice.

• *Walking*—Do walking meditation for a few minutes until sleepiness disappears. Then return to your sitting practice.

• *Splash water*—Go and wash your face with cold water.

• *Rest*—Go take a nap for a few minutes. Sometimes sleepiness actually is a sign we may need sleep.

Doubt

Symptoms: You are uncertain about what you should be doing, in the moment or in your life. There is something you don't trust. You dwell on thoughts like "What?" "Why?" "Is it right?" "Is it wrong?"

Unmindful reflection on the thoughts of what you doubt. This is what sustains doubt. Having doubts is natural. Dwelling on the doubts so that they fill your mind and give you no peace—that is not natural. The solution to dwelling on doubt with unmindful reflection is to practice mindful reflection.

Solutions: Reflect mindfully on one of the following:

• *The Buddha*—The qualities of the Buddha, the Dhamma, and the Sangha.

• *The Dhamma*—Investigate the Dhamma and watch it work. Then think about what you have read and the changes you may have seen in yourself. You gain confidence from this and your doubt weakens. When you see and investigate the truth of Dhamma, your doubt gradually fades away.

• *Past success*—Any success you have had in overcoming greed, ill will, restlessness, and sleepiness.

BREATH COUNTING TO BLOCK HINDRANCES

In Buddhist cosmology, the demon Mara personifies unskillfulness, the "death" of the spiritual life. He is a tempter, distracting humans from practicing the spiritual life by making the mundane alluring or the negative seem positive. When the hindrances arise, you can use a skillful technique to defeat these armies of Mara by counting your breath in a very special way.

Breathe in and out. Then count, "*One.*"
Breathe in and out. Then count, "*Two.*"
Breathe in and out. Then count, "*Three.*"

Go on counting this way up to *ten*. Then count down from *ten* to *one*. Count up from *one* to *nine* and back down. Count up to *eight* and back to *one*. Then count up to *seven* and back to *one*. Continue decreasing the maximum number until you get to *one*. Then stay with one for a couple of seconds.

When you do this kind of counting, hindrances interfere. They take your mind away from your calculation. As soon as you realize that you are distracted, return to the counting.

When you have returned, maybe you have forgotten what number you last counted. Or maybe you don't remember whether you were counting in ascending order or descending order. Suppose you were distracted when you were at *six*. When you return, you don't remember whether you should go from *six* to *seven* or *six* to *five*.

Just start over. With kindness toward yourself, gently reprimand yourself. Make yourself repeat the entire counting all over again from the very beginning. When this happens to you a few times, you become determined not to let your mind go here and there. Then the mind stays on your breathing and you defeat Mara. Stop when you have full confidence in yourself and in your practice. Then go back to your normal meditation exercise.

How the Hindrances Are Eliminated

How do you "kill" a hindrance? You "watch it to death." You bathe it regularly in the fiery light of awareness and it melts away. You often don't notice hindrances dying. While you are doing the awareness process there is a sense of, "It's still there. It's still there. When will it ever go away?" But one day you say, "You know, I haven't seen such-and-such around lately. I wonder why? By George, it's gone at last!" We often see it when it is present and see it when it is gone, but fail to notice that "going away" stage in which it is becoming weaker and less frequent.

The hindrances are eliminated in three stages: *Stage one* is observing moral and ethical principles and restraining the senses. During this stage, gross expression of these tendencies is prevented from arising and the senses become relatively calm. This is the stage in which you employ mindful reflection by consciously thinking about the deep nature of what is meeting your senses.

Stage two is attaining jhana, during which the five hindrances are in abeyance. At this stage, conscious thought about the nature of your perceptions does not take place. Your senses are turned inward and recognition of the fundamental nature of your perceptions is wordless and automatic.

Stage three is final and complete. It is the attainment of full enlightenment. In this stage, all underlying tendencies are uprooted from the mind.

The Fetters

The fetters are underlying tendencies in the mind that act as the roots of the hindrances. The fetters are the roots and the hindrances are their offshoots. Desert plants must absorb every drop of precious moisture from the parched soil. To do this, the root system is often enormous, much larger than the portion of the plant we can see above ground.

Fetters are also like cataracts in our eyes. When the mind is purified of hindrances by practicing jhana, it is like using eye drops to clear the eyes temporarily. But the ignorance is still there and confusion can arise again. Removal of these fetters is like surgically removing the cataracts from our eyes so that we can see perfectly again. When the fetters are removed from the mind's wisdom-eye, we can see the truth of the impermanence of all conditioned things. This leads to total freedom.

There are ten fetters, five Lower Fetters and five Higher Fetters. You will learn more about how the fetters are eliminated starting with chapter 12.

The Five Lower Fetters

Self—The view that you are a permanent self. The belief that some kind of "you-ness" lies at the center of your happiness. The idea that everything will be OK if you can get more things for "yourself" or get rid of certain situations or qualities or become different in some way.

Doubt—Fundamental doubts about the really important things, such as whether you can trust the Buddha, this Dhamma, and the Sangha. Doubts about the importance of morality. Doubts about key Buddhist doctrines such as the law of kamma and rebirth (not to be confused with reincarnation!).

Rites and rituals—The belief that you can free yourself by following set formulas and adhering to a particular belief system. Reliance on rites and rituals to do your spiritual work instead of finding the truth through your own efforts. Note that it is not just the *belief* in the rituals that does the harm, but the *attachment* to them.

Addiction to sensual pleasures—Believing that something or someone is going to come into your life and relieve the suffering that is inherent in all ordinary experience, that some pleasure will fundamentally change how you feel about yourself and the world.

Dependence upon hatred—Feeling that you can make everything all right by rejecting and attacking things.

The Five Higher Fetters

Desire for some fine material existence—Belief that continued existence in this world can relieve the inherent suffering that pervades all experience.

Desire for immaterial existence—Belief that everything will be OK if you continue to exist in some other state or place.

Conceit—Too much pride in yourself, a high and unjustified opinion of your own qualities and abilities. Self-involvement.

Restlessness—Always wanting things to change, never being satisfied with the moment.

Ignorance—Not seeing the world as it really is. Being blind to impermanence, suffering, selflessness, and the Four Noble Truths.

DESTROYING IGNORANCE WITH JHANA

The fetters can be boiled down to three underlying tendencies—*greed, hatred,* and *delusion.* Of these, delusion or ignorance is the deepest. Ignorance cannot exist by itself. It needs to be fed. Its nourishment is the hindrances. When we hold the hindrances in abeyance, we can attain jhana. Concentration then weakens our greed, and greed is the principal cause of our suffering.

Then we use our jhanic concentration to gain wisdom, the knowledge of how things are at the deepest level. With the combined power of concentration and wisdom we fully eradicate the hindrances. Then we can rip the fetter of ignorance out by the roots.

The progression goes like this: you temporarily restrain the hindrances to attain jhana; then you use jhanic concentration to gain wisdom; with the combined power of your concentration and wisdom, you eradicate the fetters and begin to eliminate ignorance more easily from the roots; concentration weakens your greed, which is the cause of suffering; finally, wisdom and concentration weaken and destroy both the hindrances and the fetters altogether; when the hindrances and fetters are destroyed, destroying ignorance is easy.

The concentration gained by overcoming the hindrances is a very healthy state of mind that can be directed to comprehend reality. Here peace, happiness, and mental health are at their peak.

This clear understanding and very powerful concentration are united as a strong team to maintain perfect mental health. This is the reason the Buddha said, "Concentrated mind sees things as they really are."

Self Talk

I spoke before about "talking to the pain." We all have negativities arise that trouble us, on and off the cushion. Holding a conversation with yourself can be a very useful tool. What follows uses physical pain as an example of the kind of self-talk that can be useful for settling the mind in many situations.

When pain arises we must talk to the pain. We must say things like this:

> This pain is not something new. I have had this kind of pain before. It vanished after a while. This pain, too, is not permanent. It will vanish.
>
> I have suffered and suffered from pain—physical and psychological—that I have experienced throughout my entire life. All of it has passed eventually. My pain is not unique. All living beings are in one kind of pain or another.
>
> I must pay total undivided attention to this pain. The Buddha advised us to use pain as an object of meditation. It is one of the four establishments or foundations of mindfulness. He has advised us to know pleasant feeling as pleasant feeling, unpleasant feeling as unpleasant feeling, neither-pleasant-nor-unpleasant feeling as neither-pleasant-nor-unpleasant feeling.
>
> I must learn to be patient. The Buddha went through an enormous amount of pain when he was practicing meditation before his attainment of enlightenment. Even after the attainment of enlightenment he had pain. Once Devadatta threw a rock at him and injured his foot. The Buddha tolerated it with patience.
>
> Pain is inevitable but suffering is avoidable. I should not suffer from pain. I should use this pain in order to get rid of suffering.

In sports they say, "No pain, no gain." And really, there is no gain without pain. It is even more so in spiritual practice. The Buddha called it "upstream swimming."

In "The Sword Simile" discourse the Buddha said,

> *Bhikkhus, even if bandits were to sever you savagely*
> *limb by limb with a two-handled saw,*
> *he who gave rise to a mind of hate toward them*
> *would not be carrying out my teaching.*
> *Herein, bhikkhus, you should train thus:*
> *"Our minds will remain unaffected,*
> *and we shall utter no evil words;*
> *we shall abide compassionate for their welfare,*
> *with a mind of loving-kindness, without inner hate.*
> *We shall abide pervading them*
> *with a mind imbued with loving-kindness;*
> *and starting with them,*
> *we shall abide pervading the all-encompassing world*
> *with a mind imbued with loving-kindness, abundant,*
>   *exalted,*
> *immeasurable, without hostility and without ill will."*

I highly recommend that you talk to the pain and the anger arising from pain in this manner. Use your own words. With a bit of thought you can modify this to other conditions that trouble you like the pain of aging or divorce or the loss of a loved one.

You can talk to your laziness. You can talk to your fear and your anger and your greed. This kind of self-talk is very useful to get control of thought chains so you can function on the cushion and to direct your life.

CHAPTER 7

The Purpose of Practice

*J*hanas can be an essential part of insight meditation. They can be used to develop the deepest possible insight into the essential features of our experiential world. The purpose of your meditation practice is to gain insight into the "three marks" of all existence: *anicca* (impermanence), *dukkha* (suffering), and *anatta* (selflessness).

Noticing changes without greed, hatred, and delusion is the essence of your mindfulness practice. Your breath and your feelings are tools. So too are your perceptions, attention, intention, and consciousness—they are all tools. They can help you understand impermanence. Once you are aware of change, you can find yourself longing for the power to stop the change. Every thought, every sensation—including the good ones, the ones you want to hang on to—they all slip away.

Unfortunately, you can't stop it. This is anicca, the impermanence of all existence.

And that makes you disappointed. You feel the unsatisfactoriness of this situation. This is dukkha, the inherently dissatisfying nature of all samsaric experience. You realize there is nothing that can stop the change, and then you also come to see there is no "myself" to do the stopping, and no essence of thing-out-there to do it to. This is anatta, the inherently selfless nature of all samsaric existence, the fact that everything you can identify as a discrete thing or activity is actually an accumulation of subcomponents and has no inherent existence of itself.

Thus, you come to experience the reality of impermanence, unsatisfactoriness, and selflessness. This is the knowledge and insight you gain from observing your own breathing, feelings, perceptions, intention, and consciousness. This is your mindfulness.

You practice it either on the cushion, or away from the cushion. You do it sitting, standing, walking, talking, and lying down. You do it while eating, drinking, wearing clothes, urinating, defecating, thinking, bending, stretching, running, writing, reading—performing any activity at all. It is all there for you to use for insight. You can notice the impermanence of anything you're engaged in, without using words or concepts to label those activities. Impermanence, unsatisfactoriness, and selflessness are not merely words or ideas. They are the intrinsic nature of all conditioned things.

This is the power of mindfulness. And jhana is where the pure truth of impermanence is seen deeply enough to carry over into all the other moments of your life.

Let's look at each of the three marks of existence in more detail.

IMPERMANENCE

Anicca is the Pali term for "impermanence" or "change." It's a word worth learning. It says more than its English translations. Anicca is not just a word or concept. *Anicca* is real. It is experience of what is actually going on in your body and mind.

Everything is changing constantly.

Yes, yes. You know this. You have heard all this before and you agree. The chair you are sitting in will one day fall apart and go to the junkyard. That is impermanence, right? Well, yes, it is. But only at the most superficial level. Knowledge of change at that level will not heal you; it will not free you; it lacks the power and clarity to carry you to liberation. Unless you gain strong concentration, you will never see it at the deep and subtle level that makes you free.

You need to sit in the place where the whole world of your experience is coming up and passing away so rapidly that there is just nothing to hang on to. Nothing lasts long enough for you to mentally glue it together into "something." As soon as you turn your attention to any occurrence, it goes "poof"! It vanishes as soon as pure awareness touches it. It all just comes up and goes away, leaving no trace. There is no time for such a trace to be left. As each thing comes up, it pushes the last thing out of the mind and there is no residue. You come out of this experience with no solid memory of anything that occurred. There is just the lingering impression of everything arising and passing away more rapidly than the mind can hold. This is termed "seeing things as they really are." You are not verbalizing or conceptualizing. You are just "seeing." This happens in the awareness of your deeply concentrated mind.

It all just comes up and goes away as a raging torrent without the slightest straw to grasp to keep you from drowning. Yet you do not drown. Because you are not really there. "Me" is just another "thing" that only exists when you glue your passing experience together in that artificial way. What does the seeing in this state is a calm, unruffled, pure *watchfulness* that does not get involved and does not exist as a thing. It just *watches*.

When you see things this way, you lose interest in trying to hold on to things. You see that it is futile and harmful and cannot lead to any truth or happiness. You lose interest in the attachment that you have to all those very, very crucially important things you worry about in your life—those things you just have to "get" in order to be happy; those worries you just have to sidestep to avoid unhappiness. It cannot be done. They are not really there to grasp or avoid. And you are not really there to do the grasping or avoiding. It is all just ceaseless change in action.

Grasping in this state is like trying to balance a tiny, tiny mustard seed on the tip of a moving needle. It is nearly impossible and why should you bother? Yet the desire is still present to grasp on to something pleasing and joyful and to run away from something disagreeable. You cannot do it and you see the futility. You realize that, "This is the nature of my life. My body, my consciousness, all my ideas and memories and attitudes and wants and needs—they are all like this—fleeting, ephemeral and fruitless. Even 'I' am like this."

WHY IS SEEING IMPERMANENCE SO IMPORTANT?

Impermanence is the slipperiest idea you have ever encountered and the most basic. It goes against everything you think you know about existence. The mind resists it both subtly and grossly. It slides into the mind easily and then slides right out again just as easily, without any impact. And it must have that impact. It is the basic idea you need to make you free.

You see things changing. You see it deeply down to the most incredibly fast, moment-by-moment level. Then you see it more broadly. You perceive it in everything you see and everything you ever could see. When you see anicca in all your experiences, your mind gets tired of this incessant change. This is the suffering, the dukkha, you experience in impermanence. This is the truth that the Buddha uncovered and expounded to us saying, "Whatever is impermanent, it is suffering."

Seeing suffering in all the aggregates of your experience, you become disenchanted. Being disenchanted you become dispassionate. Passion is the gluing nature of your mind. Passion is the glue that holds the self and the world together as apparent units of being.

When this gluing power is removed, there arises relinquishment, which leads to cessation of your suffering.

You apply mindfulness and attention without concepts. Ideas or thoughts are thorns, boils, wounds, and impediments. Without them you can focus the mind like a laser beam on the five aggregates. Then the mind can see that "I" exists only when the body, the feelings, the perceptions, the volitional formations, and the consciousness exist. They, in turn, exist within the parameters of impermanence. That burns everything. You don't find any "self" or "soul" or "I" in any of the aggregates.

Suppose you put many components together and make a flute. When you blow it, it produces a sweet sound. Suppose someone breaks this flute into little pieces. He burns each of them in search of the sound in the flute. He will never find the sound. You will never find the "I" in the aggregates. That is your discovery of anatta.

Not seeing impermanence, you tend to cling to impermanent things. You end up in suffering because impermanent things betray you when you try to hold on to them. They pull the rug out from under your feet. They deceive you. They make you believe that they are going to please you forever. They make you believe that they are going to give you permanent happiness, that your life is going to profoundly change forever when you have this solid, enduring thing or relationship or situation. They cheat you. They cannot stop changing, but they give you the impression that they will not change or pass. They tell you that you can enjoy their company forever.

When you see this undercurrent of unreality with the wisdom-eye, you are no longer confused. You no longer think they are going to make you happy forever. Seeing the impermanence of everything, you take precautions against their deceptive, constantly departing nature. At this stage, effort, mindfulness, and concentration work as a team to open your wisdom-eye so that you see everything related to the five aggregates as it really is. Supported by the luminous mind and shining with brilliant mindfulness, concentration and effort crack open the shell of ignorance. The wisdom-eye breaks in and dispels the darkness of ignorance. It sees the truth of selflessness, suffering, and impermanence as they really are.

SEEING IMPERMANENCE WITH VIPASSANA AWARENESS

There are two levels of seeing change. You can see it with vipassana awareness or with jhanic awareness. Let's look first at the vipassana experience of change.

You should begin every day with meditation, using your breath as the primary focus. As the breath becomes calm, subtle, and relaxed, the mind becomes calm and relaxed. The deeper you get into seeing this reality with unremitting energy, the more you will be filled with joy to see the truth unfolding within your experience in daily life.

Each moment is a new moment. Each moment is a fresh moment. Each moment brings you new insight and new understanding. You begin to see things that you have never seen before. You attain what you have never attained before. You see things from a totally new perspective. Each new experience brings you refreshing, calming, cooling joy and happiness.

Sometimes remarkable experiences accompany this new way of seeing the world. You may feel a calm and cool sensation spreading through your entire face, under your eyes, eyebrows, forehead, the middle of your head, and back of your head. You don't do anything artificial or deliberate to gain this happiness. It happens naturally when the conditions are ripe. Then you may experience a very subtle, very peaceful, but very sharp and clear vibration in your neck, shoulders, and chest area. As you go on breathing normally, simultaneous with this vibration, you may experience the expanding and contracting of the entire upper part of your body between the abdomen and the lower part of navel. You may experience every tiny little cell all over your body vibrating and changing, rising and falling with an inconceivable rapidity.

Not everybody feels this at the same points or in the same pattern. Some may experience this kind of phenomena elsewhere in the body or in another progression, or perhaps in a different way altogether. Do not go looking for this experience or think that something is wrong if you do not find it. The point is not the exact sequence of sensations. The point is what it means.

There is nothing static. Everything is dynamic. Everything is changing. Everything is appearing and disappearing. Feeling arises and passes away. Thought arises and passes away. Perception arises and passes away. Consciousness arises and passes away. You experience only changing. You cannot experience anything that is not changing.

Everything that you thought to be permanent is now seen to be impermanent and changing incessantly. You cannot make anything stay the same even for two consecutive moments. One moment seems to be pleasant and the mind wishes to keep it that way. Before the mind even makes this wish, it has changed. Mind moves with inconceivable rapidity. No matter how fast the mind moves to grab the pleasant experience, it changes before the mind reaches it. Its arising is like a dream. Millions of tiny little experiences arise and pass away before you blink your eyes. They are like lightening. No, much faster than that. You cannot keep up with their speed of change.

You may think, "Let me see the beginning, duration, and passing away of this experience."

Before this thought arises, the objects of your sense experience have arisen, reached their maturity and passed away. Sometimes your mind can catch the beginning of an experience. But your mind cannot see the middle or the maturity of it. Or sometimes you may experience the middle of it but not the end of it. Sometimes you may experience the end of it but not the middle or the beginning. However, you are mindful of this change. That is good. At least you can notice the changes taking place. It is even better to notice how fast they change. You experience impermanence all day long, all night long, every waking moment. In samsara, everything is "permanently" impermanent.

At this point you may feel as if you are breathing with the rest of the world. You may feel every tiny little creature from little ants to great elephants, tiny fish to the giant whales, from small worms to huge pythons. All of them are breathing to your rhythm or you are breathing to theirs.

When you mindfully pay total attention to your body, feelings, perceptions, volitional formations, and consciousness, you experience every tiny little part of them constantly changing. When your mindfulness is established, your mind notices that every split second is new. Every molecule of your body, every feeling, perception, volitional formation, and consciousness itself—they are all changing incessantly, every split second. Your breath moves in and out with this change. Your feeling keeps changing. Your experience of this change—even that experience is changing too. Your attention and your intention to pay attention to notice the change are changing. Your awareness is changing.

When you hear a sound, you experience the change in the sound. You notice the change in any sound that hits your eardrum. If you keep paying attention to it, you notice that it is slowly changing. Similarly, any smell, any taste, any touch with the body—they all change constantly. Although they change all the time, you don't know that they change until you pay attention to them.

A feeling arises that depends on sight, sound, smell, taste, touch, and thought. This also changes. Any perception that arises and depends upon sight, sound, smell, taste, touch, and thought—this also changes. Any state of consciousness that arises and depends upon sight, sound, smell, taste, touch, and thought—this also changes. When you are paying attention to them, all of them change just like when you are paying attention to your breath. Your feeling of the breath, your perception of breath, your attention to breath, your intention to pay attention to breath, and your awareness of breath—they are all changing. They rise, change, and pass without ceasing.

Seeing Impermanence in Jhana

You also need to see impermanence at a very deep level, the minute and inconspicuous changes taking place in every moment of consciousness. Before attaining jhana you know intellectually that everything is impermanent. When you experience jhana, you perceive impermanence at its most intense and subtlest level.

Before you gain right concentration, your awareness of the impermanence of all phenomena is shallow. Now it is very deep and powerful. You have left thought and sensation behind and your mind can penetrate impermanence more thoroughly than ever before. In jhana, the meditation subject as a *thing* has been left behind. The mind does not focus on any separate point beside its own collectedness. One-pointedness is the mind focusing on its own one-pointedness.

This is a preconceptual awareness, a state in which mindfulness, concentration, and equanimity work together in unison without being disturbed by any of your sensory stimuli. This is not thinking about impermanence. This is experiencing it directly. True insight wisdom comes from this experience, not from mere thinking.

What do you experience as impermanent? The jhana itself is all you see, and you see the impermanence of that. Your jhana comes and goes. The jhanic factors, like joy, happiness, equanimity, and one-pointedness, come and go and fluctuate. You clearly experience the impermanence of the jhanic factors themselves.

You see the impermanent nature of everything that fills your awareness, of all the jhanic factors. These realizations are not thoughts. They are dynamic actions or activities in the mind and body. The factors rise and fall and fluctuate and your awareness of that fluctuates along with them.

In jhana your mind is not being affected by greed, hate, delusion, or fear. At all other times words, ideas, concepts, or emotions interfere with your awareness of impermanence. Jhanic awareness is wordless. It is not thinking or speculation. It is not reflection or investigation. You have passed all that before you come to this level. This is the level where the mind sees things through the eye of wisdom. Words, thinking, investigation, or even reflection have no place. They would just get in the way. They are too slow and everything is moving too fast.

This is an experience of pure impermanence, the impermanence of the experiencing awareness itself.

SUFFERING

People ask, "Why don't we talk mainly about pleasure, joy, happiness, bliss, and peace instead of suffering?" Because suffering, *dukkha* in Pali, is important. It motivates us toward the practice that can make us truly free.

There *is*, of course, a certain degree of temporary pleasure in life. Life is certainly not without any pleasure. There is always some pleasure. But no pleasure comes without pain. What really dominates your life is not the pleasure, but the pain. Nearly everything you do in life is aimed at reducing and getting rid of this pain.

The Buddha gave a few examples of suffering. You must look at these examples impartially. If you get emotionally involved in the word "suffering," you simply suffer from your own misunderstanding and you dislike the subject without ever understanding what it is. Before we move into our discussion in detail of the jhanas, let's look directly at a few classes of suffering.

Birth is suffering. We enjoy our baby's birth. We celebrate it. Is that all we do with the baby's birth? We don't deny its pleasure and enjoyment. But is that all we have with the baby's birth? No, there are many more things.

Just imagine the amount of suffering the mother goes through during the pregnancy. Nine months she suffers emotionally and physically to take care of the fetus. Sometimes she enjoys thinking that she is going to have a baby. At the same time her anxiety is also growing. Her fear is growing. Her sense of insecurity is growing. Her discomfort is growing. The beauty she enjoys very much is changing.

At the delivery of the baby she suffers enormously. Some women die in childbirth. This is one fear many women have. They are also anxious about complications after birth. A woman never knows what kind of baby she is going to deliver—healthy, unhealthy, beautiful, ugly, intelligent, not so intelligent, one with criminal tendencies.

Once the baby is born, the mother and father must take care of the baby. They must sacrifice an enormous amount of their freedom, energy, and money to take care of the baby's education, well-being, happiness, peace, health, and general growth.

Meanwhile, is the baby totally free from suffering? Most of the time babies are born with a big cry. This cry continues throughout their lives—sometimes very loud, sometimes smoldering quietly inside them until it explodes with no notice.

Growth is suffering. Children have anxiety about growing. Adults have anxiety about growing. Children's growing is called growing and maturing. Adults' growing is called old age. At every step of growing, you have to make some adjustment, willingly or unwillingly. This adjustment is not always pleasurable. You have to accept changing situations and give up old habits. This is painful for anybody.

Sickness is suffering. You may think that sickness is suffering only when you are sick. When you are healthy you may treat a sick person in a most cruel way. You may hate the sickness. But it will come to you, too. Can you stop it with all kinds of insurance? No, you cannot stop sickness. It does not matter whether you are living in the most affluent country or the poorest country. You are subject to this. You can try to prevent some of the sickness but some comes to you whether you like it or not. This really is painful and it really is suffering.

Old age is suffering. When you are very young you may laugh at somebody when you see them trembling, walking unsteadily, talking with a tattered, wrinkled face and grey hair, not being able to cope with his own limbs. An old person cannot move as fast as he used to. He cannot talk as fast he used to. He cannot eat as much as he used to. His flesh and muscles are not as strong as they used to be. Eyesight is not good; hearing is not good. Teeth are not reliable. They fall out. They have to be replaced. He cannot do all the things he loved to do when he was young. Often there is pain. Is this not suffering?

Death is suffering. Although some people kill others, when it comes to their own death, everybody trembles. When the mind is totally distorted and in despair somebody may kill himself, but normally everybody is afraid of death. When somebody is living a long life he may say, "I am not afraid of death." This is true only when people are healthy and live long. When they come closer to death, they are afraid. We do everything to prevent death. This is the only truth we can never avoid. This is really painful and it really is suffering.

To be separated from loved ones is suffering. How many times have you experienced this reality in your own life? Have you felt this suffering when you separated from your friend? Your partner? Your parents? Your brothers? Sisters? Uncles? Aunts? Grandmother? Grandfather? Your sons? Your daughters? Your husband? Your wife? You could lose your job, or your ability to work at it. You could lose in a flood or a hurricane, for instance, all your property at once. And eventually, through trauma, disease, or, at the very least, aging, you can even lose control of your body and even your mind.

To be conjoined with an unloved one is suffering. You go to work. You have to work for somebody you hate. Is this pleasure? Your boss is very mean and giving you a very hard time. He treats you unfairly. Your landlord is very stingy. He does not fix your leaking roof. He increases your rent without giving you any additional service. Don't you think these situations are unpleasant?

Even to get what you want is suffering. Suppose you get a very expensive car. See how much you love it. But you must maintain it. You must insure it. While you are taking care of it, very much like you take care of your own life, somebody scratches it. You meet with an accident. This causes you lots of suffering.

All the five aggregates are suffering. Our aggregates—the constituents of our body and mind—are the home for all suffering. If the aggregates did not exist, no suffering would exist. The five aggregates are form, feeling, perception, volitional formations, and consciousness.

Form requires maintenance. Your body is a form. As everything is happening to the body you experience physical pain. You feel hunger so you eat. You feel the need to urinate so you urinate. You feel the need to defecate so you defecate. None of those things are very pleasant.

You experience heat, cold, and thirst. You must take care of them. You must wash the body. You must clothe it. You must take care of your physical health by eating right, exercising, and resting. You must do all these things every day.

In order to maintain this body you must have the means—money, a house, clothes, food, water, good air, and many more things. Without them you cannot maintain this body. You must work very hard to obtain all the means to support this body. This is suffering.

Feeling needs to be maintained in the same way. Every time your senses come in contact with their respective objects, this thing called feeling arises. You don't like unpleasant feeling. You always want the pleasant feeling. You always look for something that can give you happiness and avoid unhappiness. This is a real struggle. You eat, drink, sleep, rest, meditate, play games, sing, dance, and do many more things to make yourself happy. Nevertheless you still are not happy, are you? Come on, admit it. Your feelings are not easily satisfied. This is suffering.

Perception also needs to be maintained the same way. You always encounter conflicting perceptions. However you perceive something to be right now, it will change. And the change does not feel right. Somebody will come up with something that does not agree with your perception. You are in constant conflict with others with regard to your perceptions. This is suffering.

Volitional formation or thought creates more pain for you. Deciding is a problem. You think your decisions are perfect. Soon you find out somebody has made some other decision, which is approved by many and your own is looked down upon. They may think your mind is full of greed, hatred, and delusion, and with these emotional states, you have made the wrong decision. Their decisions have also been influenced by greed, hatred, fear, and confusion. Nobody seems to be able to make a clear and perfect decision. We keep changing our decisions, looking for new and better ones. This is suffering, too.

Consciousness is even trickier. You like to maintain a clear consciousness. Unfortunately, you cannot hold on to any consciousness for even two consecutive moments. As it is changing faster than the speed of light, you end up in frustration.

SELFLESSNESS

The Buddhist teaching of no-self says that the person I think I am is, in a certain way, not real, at least not in the way I conceive it and enact it in my daily life. But it's important to understand that this isn't a doctrine or a theory, it's just a description of what Buddhists generation after generation have verified as true. The "self" is an aggregation, a collection of sub-components that can be broken down endlessly. Similarly, anything your mind can identify as a discrete item is actually an accumulation. There is no real self anywhere, not in you, not in anything you sense or can identify.

The words "no-self" point to a state beyond words. In our current condition, our attention catches or snags on most of the things we feel, perceive, and think. We want some things and hate other things and ignore everything else. Our lives are spent trying to get things, avoid things, achieve things and run away from things. It all stems from a basic feeling of "I! Me! Mine!" We unconsciously think things like, "I am crucial. What I think and want and say is true and counts more than the opinions of others."

All religious traditions agree that selfishness lies somewhere near the root of our problems. No-self is a mode of perception in which "me" moves to the background and our attention flows smoothly through the world without snagging or catching on anything. Our attention is turned outward and we see things clearly. We are naturally attentive to the needs of others. We can learn this state of attention without changing our religious ideas at all.

The jhanas are particularly instructive in this respect. They are states of existence in which we move beyond our wants and needs and fears. We move into joy. We bring back peace and contentment to our lives and we find that we have not dissolved our personalities, gone crazy, or lost our souls. After that we may, if we wish, retain whatever concepts we wish about soul and afterlife and leave the philosophical hair-splitting to others.

Some historical background on selflessness may be helpful. The Buddha was born into Brahmanism, the religious context of ancient India. He saw clearly that the religion and philosophy of his society were simply not working. The doctrines were centered on the concepts of kamma and reincarnation and a hard-and-fast idea of the self, called *atman*. Religious activity was in the hands of a priestly caste called Brahmans. You needed to be born into this caste in order to interact with the gods, and the observances took the form of repetitive, empty rituals. Other castes essentially hired the Brahmans to perform the rituals. No one was getting even partially free except a few ascetics who lived in the forest and devoted themselves full time to yogic practices centered on austerities. The doctrine of atman was not setting people free. The Buddha saw this as a problem and taught the idea of *anatman* (literally, "no-self").

THE NO-SELF EXPERIENCE

So what is the experience of selflessness? It is simply the act of *not* seeing a collection of constantly shifting phenomena or perceptions as a single fixed entity. What is it really? It is actually a collection of phenomena or perceptions.

When we use the notion of self, we always use it in reference to forms, feelings, perceptions, volitional formations, and consciousness. Under very close examination, however, we don't find anything that can be identified as this "self." Although there is no such separate entity as "self," we use it as a conventional term to make our communication easy. Without using "I," "me," or "mine," our day-to-day communication becomes impossible. Just try it some time. Try to get your point across without ever referring to "me" or "I" or "mine." We need terms like "myself," "herself," "himself," or "itself" to say what we mean—and both the words and the concept of self are important for navigating the everyday world—but this does not mean that the collection of shifting things is a single fixed entity.

By seeing all forms, feelings, perceptions, volitional formations, and consciousness with the attitude, "This is not mine, this I am not, this is not my self," you can abandon the false notion of "I." It's not easy but it can be done. You can begin to escape from the delusion of self by viewing things like past, present, and future as mere conventions. Any comparative or evaluative thought is just a theory. That includes things like internal vs. external, gross vs. subtle, inferior vs. superior, and far vs. near. We have a widespread agreement to use these concepts, but that is all they are. They are concepts. You cannot find them. You cannot experience them. You can only think about them. Thinking in this way is very useful when applied to the exterior world. This is what has made humans the dominant species on the planet. But using such terms to apply to inner experience is fraught with hazards.

Have you ever *seen* Sunday or Monday? You say, "It is twelve o'clock." Have you ever seen "twelve o'clock," except on a dial in a clock? If you don't have a clock, how do you know it is twelve o'clock?

And how about the clock itself? When many parts are put together, you call it a clock. When those components are taken apart and separated, do you see a clock? No, all you see is a collection of pieces. The "clock" is a concept you use to refer to those pieces when they are put together in a particular way. You could take the same pieces and put them together some other way, to create an entirely different shape, and you would not perceive it as "a clock." The "self" is like that—a collection of components hanging together in a special way. Explore it, take it apart into its components, and it melts and disappears.

The scent of a lotus does not belong to the petals or to the stalk, or to the pistils. The scent belongs to the whole flower. Similarly, you speak of form, feelings, perceptions, volitional formations, and consciousness as "I am." You never speak of this "I am" apart from form, feelings, perception, volitional formations, or consciousness. "I am" is a concept that only applies to the entire collection of the aggregates. You only use "I" to refer to the whole assemblage when they are combined in a specific way. The notion "I am" exists in us only in relation to these five aggregates that are subject to clinging. Yet we do not regard any one thing among the aggregates as "This I am."

Suppose you send your clothes to a laundry to clean. They will clean them using various detergents. When the clothes are returned, you may find some lingering smell in the cloth. Then you put them in a sweet-scented drawer. The residual smell of cleaning vanishes. Similarly, when a person dwells contemplating the rise and fall of the five aggregates that are subject to clinging, a number of things are uprooted. The residual conceit "I am" is seen to be just that, a concept. The desire we call "mine" and the view we express as "myself" are both uprooted. They just fade, like the smell in the clothes.

At this point we have laid the groundwork in both theory and (hopefully) practice to be able to turn our full attentions to the jhanas in detail, and then later to how to cultivate and practice them.

CHAPTER 8

The Jhana States

*A*s you practice jhana-oriented meditation, you move over time through a series of mental states that become more and more subtle as you proceed through them. You start where you are now and you go far, far beyond. You move beyond the range of concepts and sensory perceptions.

All human words and concepts are tied to perception. We depend heavily on vision and hearing as our primary perceptual mechanisms. We are tied to the realm of our senses and we have never known anything else. Even our abstract concepts are based on our perceptions. When we want to say we understand something, we usually say, "I see what you mean" or "I hear you." But what does "understand" mean when applied to a realm beyond vision, hearing, or any other material sense perception?

We really cannot talk about such things with any real precision. Our normal concepts just do not apply to the non-conceptual. Yet that is where the jhana states lead and we must use words to describe it. It is the only way we know how to communicate. As we proceed through the coming description of the jhana states, words become more and more metaphorical. It cannot be helped. All we have are the concepts of our perceptual realm, but we must keep in mind that we are not really telling the full truth. Only the experience itself will reveal the truth.

There are two categories of *mundane jhanas*. The states in the first category do not have names. They are simply numbered first, second, third, and fourth jhana. These are called the *material jhanas* or the *fine material jhanas*. Those who have attained these jhanas are called "those who live happily in this very life."

The second category is known as the *immaterial jhanas* because the meditation objects of these jhanas are pure concepts, not anything material. You center your mind upon a concept until it takes you into a direct, non-conceptual experience. Those who have attained these jhanas are called "those who are liberated and live in peace."

These two categories of mundane jhanas are followed by the *supramundane jhanas*, which we shall talk about in chapter 14.

THE MATERIAL JHANAS

The material jhanas are four states of experience that lie just beyond our ordinary cognitive, sensory world, but still have some relationship to it. Normal words can be used to describe some of the events and phenomena here, but we must remember that much is metaphorical. You "see" certain aspects of your experience, but it is not visual perception.

Some people can attain liberation without the material jhanas through the path of insight meditation alone.

The First Jhana

As you enter the first jhana, something remarkable happens. There is a total break with normal thought and perception. Your mind suddenly sinks into the breath and dwells. The breath is still there, but it is no longer a "thing," just a subtle thought, much like a memory or an after-image. The world goes away. Physical pain goes away.

You do not totally lose all sensation, but the physical senses are off in the background.

Wandering conscious thoughts stop. What remains are subtle thoughts of good will toward all beings.

Your mind is filled with rapture, bliss, and one-pointedness. "Rapture" or "joy" is like the leaping elation you feel when you finally get what you have been after. "Bliss" or "happiness" is like the rich, sustained satisfaction you feel when you have it. Joy may be physical, like hair rising all over your body. It may be momentary flashes or waves that shower you again and again. Happiness is more restrained, a gentle state of continuing ecstasy.

The Buddha offered a useful simile. A man has been wandering in the desert. He is on the verge of complete collapse due to dehydration. Bliss is like drinking all he wants and soaking in a bath of cool water. Happiness is like relaxing in the shade of a tree afterward.

The first taste of jhana is usually just a flash, but then you learn to sustain it for longer and longer periods. Eventually you can experience it whenever you meditate. It lasts as long as you have decided that it should last. In the first jhana, "joy" or "rapture" predominates.

You already put the hindrances on hold and let go of normal, conscious thought as you moved into the first jhana. Now it is time to let go of other things.

The Second Jhana

In the second jhana you drop even the subtle thought of the breath. The subtle thoughts of good will drop away. Your mind is now totally free of any verbal or conceptual thoughts, even that of the breath. All that remains is a subtle reflection of thought and sensation that is more like a memory or an after-image. Joy predominates. There is happiness, mindfulness, and concentration.

The Third Jhana

It is hard to imagine that you could ever get bored with joy, but something like that takes place. Rapture is akin to excitement. It is coarse compared to the more subtle happiness and one-pointedness. Your mind turns toward bliss and one-pointedness in a way that is more delicate, refined, and stable.

Equanimity is growing. You gain a feeling of equanimity toward even the highest joy. It is just more material substance really. It is subtle, but it is still tying you to the hectic world of thought and the senses. You let it go and the joy fades away by itself.

In the third jhana, the more subtle "bliss" or "happiness" intensifies. It fills you and floods every cell of your body. Confidence rises. Mindfulness and concentration strengthen. The external world may be gone but body feeling is still present and it is wonderful. The body is very still. The breath is very gentle.

The Fourth Jhana

In the fourth jhana you go deeper still. You turn away from all mental states that would counter total stillness, even happiness. The turning away happens by itself, no effort required. Equanimity and one-pointedness get even stronger. Feelings of pain went away at the first jhana. In the fourth jhana, feelings of bodily pleasure go away, too. There is not a single thought. You feel sensation that is neither pleasant nor unpleasant. You rest in one-pointedness and equanimity. As your mind becomes progressively more still, your body and breath do the same. In the fourth jhana it feels like you have stopped breathing altogether. You cannot be roused. You emerge from the fourth jhana only at a predetermined time of your own choosing.

The fourth jhana is also the state in which mindfulness and concentration unite into an intense awareness that can penetrate deeply into the nature of existence. This is the ideal state in which to directly perceive the three primary qualities of all ordinary existence: anicca, dukkha, and anatta. You passed through jhanas one through three, simply allowing them to develop and pass. You pause at the fourth jhana. You *use* the state to see deeply into impermanence, suffering, and no-self.

THE IMMATERIAL JHANAS

The immaterial jhanas are four states that have very little relationship to our ordinary cognitive/sensory world. Normal words simply do not apply. These are called the "formless" jhanas. The first four jhanas are attained by concentration on a material form or the feeling generated by certain concepts such as loving-friendliness. You attain the formless states of the immaterial jhanas by passing beyond all perception of form.

To move into the first four jhanas, the mind turned away from one thing after another. To enter each successive formless jhana, you substitute one thing for another. You turn your attention toward ever more subtle objects of awareness. There is one-pointedness and equanimity in each of these states, but at each level they become more refined. Concentration gets stronger and steadier. No one can rouse you. You come out of jhana at a time you have predetermined for yourself.

The immaterial jhanas are not usually numbered. Each has an individual name that describes the sphere of awareness that the mind occupies or dwells upon. We give them numbers here just to show their order.

The Fifth Jhana: The Base of Infinite Space

Everything that happens in the mind can be thought of as existing "somewhere," as if in a mental space. You turn your attention away from the characteristics of whatever is in the mind and toward the "space" it occupies. This infinite space is your object of contemplation.

Anything you attend to could be likened to a signal being carried on some medium of communication. You turn your attention away from the signal and toward the carrier wave that conveys it. The mind as a space, medium, channel, or vehicle is your object of awareness.

Equanimity and one-pointedness now mature fully. You find yourself in a realm where all perception of form has ceased. You cannot be disturbed or disrupted from the outside, but the tiniest suggestion of the material senses remain. You ignore them totally, but if you turn your attention to any of them, the jhana is lost.

The Sixth Jhana: The Base of Infinite Awareness
Awareness of infinite space requires infinite awareness. You turn your attention toward that immeasurable alertness. The thought of infinite space drops away and what is left is infinite awareness without an object. You dwell in boundless consciousness, pure awareness of awareness.

The Seventh Jhana: The Base of Nothingness
The next jhana is often called the "base of nothingness." The infinite awareness of the previous jhana has no object. It is empty, vacant, and void. You turn your awareness toward this emptiness. The seventh jhana is pure focus upon no-thing-ness. Your awareness dwells on the absence of any object.

The Eighth Jhana:
The Base of Neither Perception nor Non-perception
Perception of no-thing-ness is still perception. Your mind gets bored even with that and swings away from any perception at all. Total absence of perception is sublime.

You turn your attention away from perception of the void and toward the peacefulness of total non-perception. If there is the slightest hint of desire to attain this serenity or to avoid the awareness of void, the transition will not occur.

There is no gross perception going on, yet there is still super-subtle awareness of the state itself. The eighth jhana is called "neither perception nor non-perception."

The Supramundane Jhanas

The supramundane jhana states are an absolute prerequisite to liberation. They take place at the end of both the insight meditation path and the jhana path. The supramundane is where the two paths merge.

In this series of states, the fetters, deep-rooted tendencies of the mind that bind you, are burned away without a trace. This is where the meditator does the final work of escaping from samsara.

These states sound truly remarkable and appealing, do they not? But how do we get there? We'll start to answer that question with the next chapter.

CHAPTER 9

Access Concentration

The transition point from non-jhana to jhana states is called *access concentration*. You don't find the term "access concentration" in the early Pali texts. But there *is* a state just before full concentration and we use the term "access concentration" to express that state. Access concentration is compared to the soft, weak muscles of a baby trying to learn to stand on his own feet. The baby's legs are not yet strong enough to stand, so he falls back on the ground.

You use the state of access concentration to battle and subdue the hindrances. Applying mindfulness in the state of access concentration allows you to step aside from each hindrance to deep concentration and put it temporarily on hold. Do that often enough over a long enough period and the hindrances "go to sleep." They are just mental habits and you have replaced them with the habit of mindfulness. In access concentration, the hindrances are restrained and generosity, loving-friendliness, compassion, joy, happiness, and concentration have arisen. Most meditators practice in access concentration for a good while before attaining jhana.

CHOOSING A MEDITATION SUBJECT

No single subject of meditation is suitable for every person. The Buddha recommended many different subjects of meditation to many different individuals, according to their needs. He knew that not every person makes progress at the same speed or at the same time. The Buddha has given you full freedom to determine how long you should do sitting meditation, walking meditation, lying down meditation, and standing meditation. In the entire teaching of the Buddha you can see that he always recognized individual differences and gave instructions according to these differences. He always showed how all these different methods lead to the same goal—attaining full liberation from suffering and entry into the perfect peace and bliss of emancipation. You may wish to seek the guidance of a teacher to arrive at a suitable meditation object for you.

Once that person has attained a jhana, no matter what object has been used for attaining it, the jhanic qualities are the same. The same object can also be used for both concentration meditation and insight meditation. For instance, the breath is often used for both. Pali literature mentions forty common meditation objects.

For the sake of convenience, in this book I usually describe the breath as our object of meditation. Most of what I say about the breath as a meditative phenomenon applies to other subjects, too.

A useful alternative to focusing on the breath is focusing on what is called a *kasina*. A kasina—the word means the "entirety"—is a physical object used as a meditation focus. Traditionally, these were circles used to represent certain concepts. Many were made of earth with coloring added. A traditional kasina was approximately nine inches in diameter. These objects are seldom used today, but they were a traditional method used at the time of the Buddha.

Today, *kasina* means "an object that represents a pure concept, the essence of all things with that quality." There are ten traditional kasinas, including colors and the four elements. Different people, depending on their particular inclination, use kasinas representing water, fire, air, blue, red, white, space, or consciousness. Each kasina represents a pure concept, the entire quality of something, the essence. The blue kasina represents blueness, the quality that is common to all blue objects—light blue, dark blue, royal, or aquamarine. All the shades of blue are included in this perception of blueness. Each of the kasinas represents a basic reaction in the mind, what your mind will do whenever you see anything that has the quality of blueness, yellowness, the liquidity of the water element, or any finite space.

You should select one meditation object and stay with it. Don't jump from object to object. Mixing up the object can confuse your mind. Suppose somebody asks you to dig a hundred-foot-deep hole in the ground to get water. You could dig ten holes each ten feet deep or twenty-five holes each four feet deep. You could then say logically that you have dug a hundred feet worth of holes. However, you would not get water. You should dig one hole, one hundred feet deep. Only then can you get water. Similarly, by trying all the meditation subjects, you could say logically that you have tried all of them but nothing worked for you.

When focusing on a meditation object, your objective is not to "become one with the object" and thus become deadened or stupid. Instead, you use these objects to gain a high degree of concentration by expanding each one everywhere—above, below, and across—making it undivided and immeasurable. The whole of your experiential world is filled with the quality that the kasina represents. Someone who contemplates deeply upon the earth kasina, for instance, fills his or her experiential universe with the quality of solidity. Such a person is said to be able to walk on water because the mind perceives everything everywhere as solid. Nevertheless, the person is not "one with" or "totally absorbed in" the kasina. He still perceives the external and internal universe.

Meditation objects are like launching pads. Once you have gained jhana, everything that follows after that is the same. The concentrated mind is on its own, alone, dependent upon nothing external. Whatever object has been used for abandoning hindrances and gaining concentration is left behind.

Imagine a swimming instructor encouraging a child to hold on to a kickboard in a shallow swimming pool. He wants to teach the child to float on the water. When the child is reasonably comfortable kicking in the water, the instructor slowly removes the board. Then the child gradually learns to float without the support of the kickboard. The subject of meditation is like the kickboard. It is used until the skill is built and then abandoned.

THE ENTRY POINT

If you have ever tried even a single period of meditation, you already know the initial stage. It is our normal mind.

Your focus wanders and wavers. The breath is there for you occasionally, but you keep losing it and you go off into daydreams and memories and imaginary conversations with who knows who. You notice the wandering and you pull yourself back to the focus. You fluctuate, vacillate, and swing back and forth between the breath and who knows what—distracting thoughts, feelings, and sensations.

Your first milestone comes when you detach from the world just a bit. The outer world with its sounds and sensations drifts into the background. They are still there, but they bother you less. Your thoughts are still there too, but they are quieter and they pull you away less often. You hear things, smell things, think things, but that does not disturb you so much. Some peace is present now and then. Your body becomes more and more still. You know you are headed in the right direction. Your mind begins to linger on the breath for short periods. You can feel yourself getting better at pulling it back.

This is the place where you usually start to have some real insights about your thought process. These thoughts and sensations really are annoying things! They really are disturbing. It is not a theory. The calm one-pointed focus is so much nicer. Eventually even nice thoughts are a bother compared to calm.

You start to see the hindrances too. Whether you call them that or not, you notice that certain thoughts and sensations are more jarring than others and you start learning to let them go, to let the hindrances pass without grabbing on to them.

CONCENTRATION STRENGTHENS

After a period of effort comes a noticeable strengthening of concentration. The mental attributes that will eventually mature into jhana—things like one-pointedness and bliss—become quite noticeable. This is your first major attainment. It is a state on the brink of genuine jhana. It is called "access" concentration because it is the doorway to the real thing.

Concentration is still unsteady but your mind keeps trying and it is getting easier. You fluctuate between your calm focus and your inner dialogue. You are still open to your senses. You hear and feel in the normal way, but it is off in the background. The breath is a dominant thought—an object, a thing—but it is not your sole focus. Strong feelings of zest or delight set in. There is happiness, satisfaction, and a special state of non-preference called equanimity. They are very weak, but they begin to arise. They will mature.

Your attention touches the breath repeatedly, strikes at it, flicks away and then begins to dwell upon it. You may feel lightness or floating. In the mind's eye you may see shimmering forms or flickers of light. These are not visual phenomena in the eyes. These phenomena are totally in the mind.

This is the realm of visions. If a deity or an entity is ever going to speak to you, this is where it will happen. Your normal thought patterns are being disrupted and deep imagery can come forth. Your visions may be beautiful or terrifying or just strange kaleidoscopic sequences without meaning. Whatever they are, you just let them be there and bring the mind back to the breath. They are nothing special, just more discursive thought in disguise.

ACCESS CONCENTRATION AND THE BREATH

As you continue to breathe, take note of the beginning, middle, and end of each inhalation, followed by a brief pause. Then note the beginning, middle, and end of each exhalation. This will assure that your mindfulness is strong as you approach jhana. If you do not pay careful, mindful attention, you will not be able to discern these separate stages in each breath. Each of these stages should be noticed at the place where you feel the touch of the breath. For that reason, it's very important to really find the place where the breath touches before jhana develops, and pay total mindful attention to that particular spot. By paying total attention, you also can notice the intrinsic nature of any phenomena as they arise.

As your breath becomes subtler and subtler, the details begin to be unnoticeable. Finally they disappear altogether, and the mind naturally stays only at the place where you noticed the touch of the breath. At that point, you begin to experience inhaling and exhaling as one single sensation.

Don't follow the breath all the way into the lungs or out of the nose. Just stay right with that one sensation.

The technique is like a person with a stiff neck pushing a baby on a swing. He cannot move his head, so he keeps it straight. When the swing comes right in front of him he taps it. The swing goes in the direction of his tap. When it comes back he taps it again in the other direction. It moves in the other direction. Keep your attention on the breath-spot. Do not follow the movement.

Here is another analogy. Imagine an electronic sensor mounted on a wall. Every time someone approaches this sensor, a light comes on. As soon as the person has passed by, the light goes off. Similarly, every time you inhale or exhale, your mind notices the sensation of your inhaling or exhaling at the place where the breath touches. It simply registers the sensation without following the movement.

Each time the mind wanders away from the breathing, you bring it back and keep it at the touch-point. Repeat that process, as often as necessary, until the mind stays easily with the breath, as it flows in and out, passing the place where you established your attention. Then you will be able to see every tiny part of the breath.

As you watch every part of your breath, it eventually becomes subtler and subtler until you cannot even notice its movement. All you notice is a strong but pleasant sensation at the place where you established your attention. First the mind lets go of noticing the beginning, middle, and end of the breath. Then the mind focuses only on the inhaling and exhaling. Finally, even the subtle breath is replaced by just that strong sensation at the touch-point.

Breathing in and out, you experience the feeling of your breath. And as the breath changes, so does the feeling. You perceive the changing breath and the changing feeling. The thought, "This is the breath—this feeling, this perception," is called *volitional formation*. You intentionally (or "volitionally") pay attention to the breath and its sensations. Your awareness or consciousness also changes as your breath, feeling, perception, and thought change. You realize that any state of consciousness also changes, whether it arises dependent upon sight, sound, smell, taste, touch, or thought.

While noticing the impermanence of breath, if the mind goes to a sound, notice the impermanence of the sound. Ignore your emotional or conceptual response to it. Just spot the impermanence. It comes and it goes. There is sound and then silence.

If the mind swings to a feeling, notice the impermanence of that feeling. If your mind fastens on a perception, notice the impermanence. If the mind goes to your own attention, notice the impermanence of attention itself. In other words, you pay attention to the impermanence of everything you experience, even your own paying attention. When the mind becomes stable and does not go to anything other than the breath, you stay with the breath and notice the impermanence of that alone.

When all the hindrances have subsided, joy arises. Develop that joy further and let go of your restlessness. Let the joy spread all through your mind and body. This is a right thought, too.

Pin your attention to the simple sensation of breath at the nostrils. Stay with it as the breath naturally slows down and becomes fine and light. Allow thoughts of the breath to drop away. Stay with the simple sensation. Just let the process happen. Don't try to rush it.

Approaching the First Jhana

In access concentration some interesting phenomena take place. People report dreamlike experiences and strange sensations of rising or floating or flowing. Some people report visions, but you should neither chase after these kinds of things, nor worry if they do or don't come. Your attention is coming back to the object of meditation again and again, touching it and swinging away, then hovering around it closer and closer. As the first jhana approaches, there is a stage when your attention "sinks into" the meditation subject.

You attain the first jhana with the beautiful pleasant feeling arisen from having restrained hindrances and practicing metta. Your joy and happiness arise from being separated from all your physical worldly activities and from the hindrances that arise from those things. Now you can take a deep breath and relax. You can sit down quietly and enjoy the solitude and peace.

Even though your concentration in the first jhana is not very deep, you enjoy the freedom from all the hustles and bustles of worldly life. Concentration and equanimity are there too, though these two factors are not prominent in the first jhana. There is also one-pointedness or unification of mind. In the first jhana the joy and happiness you feel arise from seclusion and from the absence of the hindrances.

Some teachers lay a lot of emphasis on the importance of using the sensation of delight as a tool to enter jhana.

They recommend that, if you feel this delight only in one location, you should enlarge it. The whole body should be bathed and saturated with the feeling of bliss. This is a physical sensation, though not the kind that you are familiar with in ordinary life. It is similar to an extremely pleasurable sensory phenomenon, but not identical, far more subtle and gratifying.

You can take control of this feeling and, to some extent, direct it. Once you have learned to concentrate, you can get to the delightful sensation any time you wish and stay in it as long as we wish.

For instance, when doing the metta meditation described in chapter 4, feelings in the center of the chest may occur. This is usually a very enjoyable feeling of bodily warmth. As soon as it comes, you should let go of the metta practice, place your entire concentration on the sensation, and expand it to suffuse the entire body. This physical feeling is similar to the more subtle feelings of joy and bliss in jhana. This feeling can be used as a bridge to allow you to slide naturally into jhana.

When you have taken care of all the hindrances, the breath

becomes very subtle. You may not even feel it. You may think it has stopped. There is nothing to worry about. It is still going on. When all the disturbing factors are gone, the mind returns naturally to the breath. When breath becomes subtle enough that it is unnoticeable, your mind focuses on the memory of this subtle breath as your object for gaining concentration.

Watch for the sensation to change into a kind of vivid after-image. Stay with that. Keep at it. Be persistent. This memory may then be replaced with a little spark of light. If so, that becomes your focus of attention. This is a very important moment, the moment just before true concentration. This spark is your signal. You are about to enter jhana.

At the beginning there may be just a fleeting experience that can be very hard to identify. The first time there may be just a strange, indefinable discontinuity that often evokes a startled, "What was that? What just happened?" Do not question such experiences. Any verbalized pondering will just lead you away from the goal. Just stay with your concentration practice. If some strange experience arises that you think might be jhana, pay no attention. When real jhana arises, you will know what it is.

If all goes well, in the next moment after experiencing the spark, you gain genuine jhanic concentration and hold it. There are thoughts of generosity, friendliness, and compassion that you have already cultivated by overcoming greed, hatred, and cruelty. They are not really "thoughts." You experience just the shadow of the generosity, friendliness, and compassion that are holding greed, hatred, and aversion at bay. The joy, happiness, and concentration in jhana have restrained drowsiness, restlessness, and doubt.

CHAPTER 10

The First Jhana

When you enter the first jhana you are still in touch with your physical senses. Your eyes are closed but you can still hear, smell, feel, and taste. This is one definite indication of the first jhana, as opposed to others.

You don't fully lose thought either. Thoughts come now and again. Since you have been thinking all your life, your thoughts do not disappear all of a sudden at the attainment of the first jhana. They are like nervous habits—difficult to wipe out at once. They continue to haunt your mind periodically. Just ignore them. They are one of the things that will pull you out of jhana. You want to be able to maintain it as long as you wish.

This passage describes the moment you enter the first jhana with all the jhanic factors and qualities:

> Quiet, secluded from sense pleasures, secluded from unwholesome states of mind,
> one enters and dwells in the first jhana,
> which is accompanied by applied thought and sustained thought,
> with rapture and happiness born of seclusion.

A DIFFERENT KIND OF JOY

When you finally overcome the five hindrances, you experience a great relief. This relief slowly increases until it culminates in *piti*, joy. This joy is purely internal. It does not arise dependent on worldly or household pleasure. Nothing outside you causes it. It arises through renouncing outward pleasure.

This joy is called "non-sensual joy." It does not gush into the mind suddenly. You have been experiencing pain arising from the hindrances for a long time. You have been working very hard to overcome those that have caused you pain. Now, every time you overcome one of them, you experience a great relief that that particular pain has subsided. It is this relief, this freedom from that particular hindrance, that brings you joy. Now you no longer have the pain caused by that particular hindrance. It is gone. You rejoice.

This is the state that the Buddha explained to Ajatasattu in the Samaññaphala Sutta:

> But when he sees that these five hindrances
> have been abandoned within himself,
> he regards that as freedom from debt,
> as good health, as release from prison,
> as freedom from slavery, as a place of safety.

> When he sees that these five hindrances
> have been abandoned within himself, gladness arises.
> When he is gladdened, rapture arises.
> When his mind is filled with rapture,
> his body becomes tranquil.
> Tranquil in body, he experiences happiness.
> Being happy, his mind becomes concentrated.

Because the hindrances have been overcome, your joy continues to increase. It arises cumulatively, slowly filling up the entire mind and body. This is the stage where you feel that your entire body and mind are diffused with joy and happiness like sugar or milk or salt mixed with water.

The ordinary, material joy we are accustomed to arises from contacting things that are desired, agreeable, gratifying, and associated with worldliness. They are simple, basic things like seeing forms, hearing sounds, smelling smells, tasting tastes, touching tangibles, and thinking mind-objects. This is called *joy based on the household life.*

When you seek and know the impermanence, the change, the fading away, and the cessation of all these things, a different joy arises. You perceive the forms, sounds, smells, tastes, touches, and mind-objects as they actually are. You see with proper wisdom. You know they are all impermanent, suffering, and subject to change. You see that they are like this now and that they always were. Then a new joy arises. This is called *joy based on renunciation.*

So you overcome joy based on the household life by the joy based on renunciation that is attained in jhana. You can overcome grief based on the household life by the grief based on renunciation, too. You can grieve for the loss of your dog or your car or you can grieve over the unsatisfactoriness of all phenomena. One leads to further involvement with the source of grief and the other leads away from that involvement.

You overcome equanimity based on the household life by equanimity based on renunciation. Although equanimity is the ideally balanced state of mind, as long as it arises based on household life, it still is diversified. It is conditioned by individual things and circumstances. But the equanimity that arises in jhanic attainment is unified. It is based on the natural unity or one-pointedness of mind. It is based on concentration. This is the highest kind of equanimity.

To regard all your children as exactly equal and treat them all just the same is a wonderful worldly goal. To regard every experience—good or bad—as equal lies beyond that.

THE FIVE JHANIC FACTORS

Mindfulness is present in your jhana. You are awake. You notice (mindfulness) and recognize (clear comprehension) the components of your own experience. You do not notice the external world, but you are fully awake to the jhanic factors that comprise your internal experience. You are mindful of what is present, the five jhanic factors.

A "factor" is a feature or aspect of something. It is a dynamic thing, often a cause of something else, often something you must do or have to make that second thing come into existence. In this case, it is something that must be present for enlightenment to take place. It is also a quality that every enlightened being displays.

These five factors hold the first jhana together: *Vitakka*—Laying hold of a thought with applied attention. It is a directed thrust of the mind, a turning of attention toward a meditation subject, such as the right thoughts of renunciation, loving-friendliness, and compassion. Some English translators have called vitakka "initial thought," but not in the normal sense of those words. Vitakka lies beyond normal "monkey mind" cognitive thought. It is likened to the striking of a bell.

Vicara—Maintaining right thoughts with sustained application. Often rendered as "discursive thought," vicara is the mind roaming about or moving back and forth over thoughts. It is a sustained dwelling upon the meditation subject. It is likened to the reverberation or resounding of the bell after it is struck.

Piti—Sometimes translated as "joy," "rapture," "enthusiasm," "interest," or "zest." It is not a physical feeling. It may be described psychologically as "joyful interest." A high degree of piti is present is the first few jhanas. It is strongest in the second jhana.

Sukha—Sometimes translated as "happiness," "pleasure," or "bliss." It may be either a physical or a mental feeling. Sukha is an indispensable condition for attaining jhana. It is present in the first, second, and third jhanas and is strongest in the third.

Ekagatta—One-pointedness; unification of mind. It implies serenity and tranquility as well as single-pointed concentration.

RIGHT THOUGHTS

Let's look more closely at the first two jhanic factors, vitakka and vicara.

In the first jhana, three *right thoughts* must be cultivated with applied thought (vitakka) and their opposites must be abandoned. When maintained with sustained application (vicara), these thoughts will become perfectly pure at the attainment of the supramundane jhanas and full enlightenment.

In jhana, these right thoughts buffer the mind, hold the hindrances at bay, and keep them from entering. They have the function of guarding the mind without clinging, keeping it steady and peaceful. This is not the kind of guarding where you hold something to your chest to keep anyone else from taking it. That is greed. This is a gentle, non-grasping function. What you are guarding is your own greedlessness. You hold it gently, like a baby.

The three right thoughts are renunciation, loving-friendliness (metta), and non-cruelty (compassion). Let's look more deeply at each.

The First Vitakka: Renunciation

Renunciation begins with the thought of generosity. You are not attached to worldly wealth, position, and power. You renounce them.

You let them go. You give them away. You do not need them and you are happier without them.

The first step toward practicing generosity is giving up the desire to hold on to your trivial material possessions. This is what you do every time you let go of some petty thing and give it away for someone else to enjoy.

The second step is to cultivate the thought of abandoning your indulgence in sensual pleasure in both words and deeds. This is what you do temporarily when you go off to a meditation retreat. This is what you do in miniature every time you sit to meditate.

The third step is cultivating the thought of not getting involved with sensual pleasures, at least during your meditation. Abandoning the thought of desire for sensual pleasures by cultivating the resolve toward renunciation is called *factorial replacement*. It is replacing one thing with another, smothering one impulse by instilling its opposite.

Before he attained enlightenment, the Buddha divided his thoughts into two classes. He put the thoughts of sensual desires, thoughts of ill will, and thoughts of cruelty in one class and the thoughts of renunciation, friendliness, and compassion in the other class. When he noticed that one of the thoughts belonging to the negative category arose in him, he became fully aware of it and mindfully reflected that this particular thought was harmful to him, harmful to others, and harmful to both. Then that particular thought subsided. When another unwholesome thought arose in him, he used the same technique to overcome that thought. By this "mindful reflection" he abandoned negative thoughts one by one.

On the other hand, when thoughts of renunciation, friendliness, and compassion arose in him, the Buddha became mindful of their arising. Then he reflected that these thoughts aid wisdom. They do not cause difficulties. When he spent days and nights reflecting on these wholesome thoughts, the Buddha felt secure. There was no longer anything to fear from their opposites.

The Buddha's instruction is that you should do the same. As a result of the right thought of renunciation, the mind becomes very calm, relaxed, and peaceful. It has no concern for anything in the world. You just let things go. You pay no attention. Your clinging and craving for ordinary things subsides.

The Second Vitakka: Loving-Friendliness

You have seen the danger of ill will. You have been cultivating the habit of not harboring ill will toward anybody. You have learned from experience how much you have suffered from your own ill will and that of others. After applying appropriate remedies you have succeeded in letting go of your anger and cultivating loving-friendliness. You take another deep breath of relief.

Generally, the last hindrance to leave the mind is hatred. When it is gone, metta arises naturally. The void is filled with feelings of friendliness toward everyone. When you no longer push things away, you naturally feel close to everything. You feel positive toward everybody. Everybody is your friend.

The Third Vitakka: Non-Cruelty

With the arising of this, you are now very glad that you are no longer cruel to people or animals. You have seen beings suffering from cruelty. You know quite well how animals and people suffer at the hands of cruel people. Having witnessed for yourself other people's cruelty, you may have felt the pain of the victims in your own heart. So you have decided not to be cruel and to cultivate compassion for all living beings.

Now you are totally at peace. You feel totally secure. You have no fear that anyone will hurt you. Thoughts of cruelty fade and you no longer have any desire to hurt or punish anyone. The natural result is compassion. You naturally feel and identify with the struggles others are going through and you have a natural desire to help them however you can. Your heart pours out to suffering beings everywhere.

THE IMPORTANCE OF VITAKKA AND VICARA

Your vitakka in the first jhana is turning toward these three thoughts. They stay (vicara) in the mind, continuously supporting the first jhana.

Note the role of conscious thought in this progression. We use conscious thoughts, such as thoughts of loving-friendliness, to pervade the mind and push away hindrances. When the hindrances have been restrained, we carry the subtle residue of loving-friendliness into jhana. All the vitakkas work that way.

Note also that we must actually work at these vitakkas, applying considerable effort at the beginning to establish a firm ethical ground. You cultivate these conceptual thoughts day and night, on the cushion during formal meditation and off the cushion in your daily life. In your meditation work you make a conscious effort to replace unhealthy conscious thoughts with healthy ones. You replace unwholesome vitakkas with wholesome vitakkas. You root out greed, hatred, and cruelty and replace them with thoughts of letting go, loving-friendliness, and compassion for others. They become a wholesome habit that naturally permeates your jhana. The subtle remnants of these conscious thoughts prevent greed, hatred, and cruelty from invading your jhana.

Nevertheless, this is not some giant struggle. You cannot get these effects through straining. You simply cultivate the ground, and the seeds grow by themselves. After establishing a solid ethical foundation for your life and cultivating these wholesome thoughts, you reap the reward. Your mind is peaceful. You feel a great gladness in having given up your hectic, grasping ways. You feel secure. You feel that you have an infinite number of friends. This is the fertile ground that grows concentration.

When verbalized vitakkas turn into real, pure mental activities, they become jhanic factors. In jhana, most normal, conscious thoughts have been left behind. There are no more words.

"Thought" in Jhana

In English the word "thought" is always used to mean normal cognitive thinking, like "thinking" about what you will buy at the store. In Pali there is a whole range of words that can be translated into English as some kind of thought or component of the thinking process. We just don't have the terms to express these tiny but important differences unless we spend a lot of time learning a whole range of very subtle concepts.

It is probably easiest to understand the nature of "thought" in jhana if we speak first of using a kasina, a physical object, as our meditation subject. You start out by looking at the physical object. Then you shut your eyes and bring it to mind as a visual image. Eventually the object comes fully into focus when you attend to it with eyes shut. It is as clear as when you look at it with eyes open. This is your *learning sign*. You stop gazing at the physical object and focus solely upon the learning sign. You develop it by striking at it over and over with vitakka (applied thought) and maintaining it with vicara (sustained thought). It then turns into something more subtle, like an after-image. This is called the *counterpart sign*.

As you practice this way, the *jhanic* factors grow in strength, each restraining its respective hindrance. Applied thought, for instance, counters sloth and torpor, eventually reducing it to a state of complete abeyance. When the hindrances are restrained and the defilements subside, your mind enters access concentration. This is when the learning sign is replaced by the counterpart sign.

The *Visuddhimagga*, an ancient commentary on the path of meditation, explains the difference between the learning sign and the counterpoint sign like this:

> *In the learning sign, any fault in the kasina is apparent. But the counterpart sign appears as if breaking out from the learning sign. It is a hundred times, a thousand times, more purified. It is like a looking-glass disk drawn from its case, like a mother-of-pearl dish well washed. It is like the moon's disk coming out from behind a cloud, like cranes against a thundercloud. But it has neither color nor shape, for if it had, it would be gross, cognizable by the eye, susceptible to comprehension by insight. But it is not like that. It is born only of perception in one who has obtained concentration, being a mere mode of appearance.*

The counterpart sign is the object of both access concentration and jhana. The difference between access concentration and the first jhana consists, not in their object, but in the strength of their respective *jhanic* factors. In access concentration the *jhanic* factors are still weak and not yet fully developed. In jhana they are strong enough to actually thrust the mind *into* the object with the full force, like a carpenter pounding a peg into wood or a stone sinking into water. In this process *applied thought* (vitakka) is the factor most responsible for bringing about the mind's sinking into the counterpart sign.

In metta meditation and elsewhere we speak of "thoughts" of loving-friendliness in jhana. Applied thought *in* jhana is associated with wholesome roots. It takes the form of wholesome "thoughts" of renunciation, benevolence, and harmlessness. What is the nature of these thoughts? You have to experience it to really understand. Words can only approximate. You use conceptual thoughts of metta to develop physical feelings. Then you turn your attention to the feelings and discover a subtle "color" or "flavor" in the mind that is the pure, non-conceptual feeling of metta. This is what you use to carry you into jhana and this *vitakka* is what you carry with you into jhana.

When using the breath as your object of focus, you use conscious thoughts to help you direct your attention onto the breath. You find the physical feeling. You drop conscious thought and dwell purely on the feeling. This is your learning sign. A spark of light sometimes appears. This signals the arising of your counterpart sign. The subtle after-image of the physical feeling of the breath is what you carry with you into jhana.

THE SEVEN FACTORS OF AWAKENING

One of the most important aspects of the first jhana is that at this point, you begin your progress toward liberation through a succession of seven stages. Each stage leads to the next. They take place in the same order for each of us. No one ever skips any stage. Each stage is a natural outgrowth of the one before. These seven stages culminate in the attainment of *sotapanna*, "stream entry," the first stage of enlightenment. In each stage you develop a "factor of awakening."

The First Factor: Mindfulness
You need mindfulness to build jhana, but what is the proper domain for your mindfulness? What is your frame of reference in meditation? What do you concentrate on? You can't get jhana through concentrating on just anything. You must use certain specific subjects in your meditation. They must be things that promote dispassionate observation and reveal the truth of anicca, dukkha, and anatta.

Those proper objects of focus, the *four foundations of mind-fulness*, are described in the *Satipatthana Sutta*. When using each object you must remain "ardent, alert, and mindful, putting aside greed and distress with reference to the world." That means you put some effort into the thing, do it with zest and vigor. Pay mindful attention to what you are doing and leave your day-to-day bothers behind while you are doing it. The four foundations of mindfulness constitute the basis and the guiding principles of concentration.

Mindfulness of the body focuses your attention on the body itself and its position and movement. You see that breathing is something that takes place within the body itself.

Mindfulness of feelings focuses on physical sensations. You watch them, looking constantly for their deeper nature, the way they are constantly changing and have no real substance other than what you give them with your mind. Tactile sensation is a feeling. Hearing is a feeling, too, if you ignore the other mental content that arises with it and just concentrate on the pure sensation of sound vibrations. The same is true for all the senses.

Mindfulness of consciousness focuses on watching thoughts and emotional reactions arise without getting involved in them. That includes things like discursive thoughts, internal conversation, pure concepts, and mental pictures. You see them as bubbles just coming up and going away without any particular meaning. You don't take them seriously.

Mindfulness of mental objects focuses on seeing the inherent nature of your whole experience: *anicca*, *dukkha*, and *anatta*. You face directly, in real time, the changing nature of everything you experience and everything material that you can experience. You see that none of it makes you really happy and that you are not really a somebody who is stuck in it all.

You can and must think about these things. That is valid practice. But remember that all such thoughts exist to guide you to the goal of the wordless experience of these things as the truth, exactly the way it is.

Mindfulness of impermanence in any of the four foundations is the entry point. Seeing anicca leads you to seeing dukkha and anatta. Seeing these three marks of existence leads you to liberation.

The Second Factor: Investigation

Out of mindfulness arises investigation.

While being mindful of the impermanence, unsatisfactoriness, and selflessness of one thing, the mind inevitably swings to some other thing. When that happens, you investigate that new object more closely, wordlessly looking for the impermanence, wordlessly asking, "Is this permanent or impermanent?" As you ponder that question and pay more mindful attention to this new object, you will see it as impermanent, unsatisfactory, and without self.

Can any object be permanent? The answer is "No." But don't take my word for it. Investigate for yourself.

Then you must investigate your mind and body with another question in mind: "Where can I find something permanent in this mind and body, with its perceptions, thoughts, feelings, and consciousness?" The answer will be, "Nowhere." But hearing this will not change you. You need to perform the investigation yourself, sincerely and exhaustively.

Concentration holds an object before mindfulness. Mindfulness then pays close attention to it. Then investigation finds that it is constantly changing, thus showing the signs of unsatisfactoriness and selflessness.

The Third Factor: Energy

Out of investigation arises energy.

This investigation arouses your energy to look for anything permanent and push away anything impermanent. Deeper mindfulness and investigation arouse stronger effort to see deeper, subtler aspects of anicca, dukkha, and anatta. Because this energy is aroused, you never tire in your mindfulness. You investigate the nature of impermanence, suffering, and the selflessness of your body. You delve into your feelings, perceptions, thoughts, and consciousness where you find the same thing. You do it with a vigor born out of spiritual urgency. You never tire of seeing tiny, perhaps even molecular, changes in the breath. Your effort helps you make progress.

This is the power of the energy factor of enlightenment. You have a natural energy in jhana. It carries over into your normal life, too.

The Fourth Factor: Joy

Out of energy arises joy.

Suppose you are traveling in a desert. You are hungry, thirsty, tired. You are full of worries, full of doubt as to where you should go. You need to get water, food, shade, and help. A man appears. His hair and clothes are dripping with water. Where did he come from? Where did he get this precious water you need so desperately?

You ask him. He points. He says, "Continue walking that way and you will find a forest. Right there, in a clearing in that forest, there is a natural lake."

You continue in the direction he pointed. Then, from a distance, you hear birds singing. You hear animal noises and people talking. As you get closer and closer, you hear people jumping into the water, swimming, and playing. As you get still closer you see all kinds of birds, animals, and human beings—boys, girls, teenagers, adults, old people. They are bathing, swimming, eating water lilies, lotus buds, lotus roots. They are drinking the water and relaxing on the bank of the lake. Seeing all this, your joy and gladness intensify.

Then you jump into the lake. You swim in it, play with the water. You drink all you want. You eat the delicious lotus roots and the water lilies. You frolic in the lake for hours. Then you come out of the water and stretch your arms and legs. You lie down on your back saying, "What happiness. I am happy! I am truly happy!"

In this image, the gladness that arises in your weary mind when you see that fresh lake is like the joy that arises in your mind in meditation. As you are approaching the lake and hearing the sounds coming from it, your joy increases by degrees. When you jump into the water and drink, you are absolutely delirious with joy. As you eat the lotus roots and water lilies, you experience a deep tranquility. When you came out of water and relax on the beach you are relaxed and happy, deeply content. It might even put you to sleep.

Similarly, in jhana, joy arises slowly and increases until it turns into tranquility and happiness. Normally you may use these two words—joy and happiness—to indicate states of excitement. Ordinarily, when you are excited you may jump up and down. You smile. You laugh. You hug someone. You talk a lot. You sing. You kiss someone you love. You dance and even cry out of such excitement. While expressing your excitement through all these activities, you may say, "I am happy." But this is not the happiness of jhana. Jhanic happiness is calm, peaceful, and smooth. It is not excitement. It is almost the opposite. Spiritual happiness makes you relaxed, calm, peaceful, and concentrated.

Sometimes, even in meditation, your eyes may be filled with tears when you are full of this deep joy. But, if you are mindful, you can become fully aware of your joy without shedding tears, without a murmur or a movement.

Once you have achieved the joy factor of enlightenment, you automatically feel so much loving-friendliness and compassion for all beings that a natural wish arises in your mind: "May all living beings live in peace and harmony!" When practicing this mindfulness of loving-friendliness, this compassion for all living beings, you appreciate whatever you have. You experience appreciation of whatever others enjoy, and you feel extremely grateful for everything you have received.

This is the power of joy. The joy of jhana carries over into a joy in your normal consciousness. It is a joy that fuels your life.

The Fifth Factor: Tranquility

Out of joy arises tranquility.

The calm, cool, and refreshing joy engendered by this practice makes your mind and body calm, relaxed, and peaceful. When the mind is calm and peaceful, you feel serene and tranquil. You are satisfied. The fever of anger is cooled. The fire of lust has subsided. Delusion is dispelled. Grief, pain, sorrow, lamentation, and despair have all disappeared. You no longer feel the burning of jealousy, fear, tension, anxiety, and worry. Instead, you feel safe and secure. Although you have not yet achieved your final goal, at this level you have temporary peace and happiness.

The power of the deep peace of jhana carries over. It begins to pervade your life. You live and practice your mindfulness with an ever-deepening tranquility.

The Sixth Factor: Concentration

Out of tranquility arises concentration.

The Buddha said, "One who is happy gains concentration. One whose mind is filled with loving-friendliness gains concentration very quickly." In the first jhana, your thoughts of friendliness, compassion, generosity, equanimity, joy, and happiness are very strong. They hold your attention effortlessly.

What creates this unification of mind, this one-pointedness? It is hard to say in words, but analogies may help. Imagine that in the distance there are mountains, traditionally, thirty-seven peaks and ridges, corresponding to the thirty-seven factors of enlightenment—things like the Noble Eightfold Path, and the four foundations of mindfulness. These merge into seven major mountains, the seven factors of awakening. Their peaks are in the clouds. A fine drizzle is falling constantly. Tiny, tiny drops of water are showering down gently nearly all the time. Occasionally it rains harder. Drops are continually accumulating. Each of these drops is a tiny moment when one of the factors dominates your mind. We all have fleeting flashes of things like mindfulness, concentration, and certainty that what we are doing is right. This is a state of scattered mind. The factors you want to be unified are occurring in rare fits and starts.

These tiny mind-moment droplets seep into the ground, percolate through the soil and are purified. Harmful elements are filtered out and healthy minerals percolate in. The drops flow together, merge and surface as tiny springs. The springs create rivulets that flow together into streams. The streams flow together into creeks. This process continues and the water is rushing down the mountain, singing as it goes over rocks and crashing as it plunges in water-falls. Every drop is laden with the potential factors of enlightenment accumulated within it. Eventually they form a mighty river, a huge river, like the Mississippi or the Nile or the Ganges.

But the power of this river is harnessed. Someone has been very clever and dammed the river where it flows through a gorge. It forms an enormous lake, a really big lake like Lake Superior or the Caspian Sea. The lake contains all the power of all the droplets that fell on the mountains, stored as potential energy in the weight of the water. Innumerable tons of water press against the dam, trying to release their power. Your mind is still scattered, but less so. The factors have gained great potential power through being unified, but the power has not yet sufficiently concentrated to create the effect you want.

Someone has been even more clever. They have put holes in the dam, small holes compared to the huge volume of water trying to pour through them. The water gushes with enormous force as it squeezes its way through those holes, turning its potential energy into the kinetic energy of movement. Now your mind is no longer scattered. The factors have been unified to release their power. Their power is now the power of concentration.

There are turbines mounted in the path of the raging flow. They spin huge generators, which convert the kinetic energy into electrical energy, enough power to light Canada or a whole section of Europe. This concentrated power flows through electric lines to light bulbs in cities and homes. It is the bright flame of mindfulness that reveals the luminous nature of the mind. With this much power behind it, mindfulness blazes through the accumulated dirt of lifetimes and produces liberation. Concentration has accumulated tiny mind-moments in which the various factors expressed themselves singly into a state in which they are all present together, constantly.

In this state of mind, with jhanic concentration, you continue to pay total attention to your experience of change. Your awareness of impermanence is much sharper and clearer than ever before because it is backed by right concentration. Previously, before you gained right concentration, your awareness of the impermanence of all phenomena was shallow. Now it is very deep and powerful. Your mind can penetrate impermanence more thoroughly than ever before.

This time you see not only impermanence, but also the fact that everything impermanent is unsatisfactory. Your mind gets tired of clinging to any pleasant experience, because the experience inevitably changes before the mind even reaches it. Even your mindfulness is changing. You may even begin to feel bored with it all. Keep watching this boredom. You will notice that the boredom is also changing. The meditation subject, as a thing, has been left behind. The mind does not focus on any separate point beside its own collectedness. One-pointedness is the mind focusing on its own one-pointedness.

This power of jhanic concentration makes everything you do and think deeper. You apply the concentration in your daily life off the cushion and it takes your mindful investigation of everything to a higher level. You see more easily into the impermanence, suffering, and selflessness of everything you are doing.

Concentrated mind sees things as they really are. You become deeply disappointed with the mental rubbish you have been making and holding on to. You let it go at last. And then you are free.

The Seventh Factor: Equanimity

Out of concentration arises equanimity.

Once you can see that all of the components of the body and mind—in the past, present, and future—are impermanent, unsatisfactory, and selfless, something remarkable happens. Equanimity arises regarding all conditioned things. Your mind looks at everything with equanimity—wholesome, unwholesome, physical, verbal, and mental. Good, bad, or indifferent, it is all the same. It is being-ness. It is simply reality. Your viewpoint is imperturbable.

Then you feel a spiritual urgency. You accelerate your mindfulness practice and do it even more vigorously. When you are in this state of mind, you have deeper insights into the Noble Eightfold Path. You use your mindfulness, your concentration, and your attention to recognize impermanence. You study and pierce unsatisfactoriness and selflessness in the body and mind. You realize that all those "wonderful" thoughts and feelings are constantly changing on a very subtle level—and the "terrible" ones are constantly changing, too.

CHAPTER 11

The Second and Third Jhanas

*I*n your upward movement in any spiritual practice, you encounter obstacles. You must struggle with these to go to the next higher attainment. You must let go of your lower desires to secure what you have attained. It has to be done without greed in order to proceed with greater perseverance. It is like climbing a ladder. You must let go of the lower rung that you are standing on and securely hold on to the one you have grabbed. You must lift one foot to step on the higher rung. It takes a willingness to let go. If you feel comfortable with the rung you are standing on and cling to it, you can't climb another step. You are stuck on the first rung of the ladder.

> *Knowing this body to be like a clay pot,*
> *Establishing this mind like a fortress,*
> *One should battle Mara with the sword of insight,*
> *Protecting what has been won,*
> *Clinging to nothing.*

This is the situation you are in when you have attained the first jhana. Joy and happiness have arisen from abandoning hindrances. Being away from all worldly affairs is wonderful. This is a very enticing and attractive situation. Sensual desire is left behind, so becoming attached to that is not possible. Nevertheless, genuine peace, joy, and happiness are unimaginable while you are involved in worldly affairs. Now you have something you never had before. This is an ideal state in which to get stuck.

The *Dhammapada* stanza quoted above says the body is like a clay pot. It is very fragile. It can break any time. In order to protect it, the Buddha advises us to build a fortress around it with the mind. The mind is even more fragile, delicate, fast changing, fickle, and unsteady. But, building this wall with such a mind, you are asked to fight Mara and gain some ground. Once you have gained ground, then you must protect it without attachment to it. That is hard.

When you are attached to something, you protect it. If you don't attach to something you let it go. The Buddha advised us to protect what you gained without attachment. This is the nature of spiritual achievement. If you are attached to the jhana you have attained, you cannot make progress. Nor can you make use of it. In order to protect your fragile body, you must use the even more fragile mind and build a fortress around it to fight Mara. These two fragile objects should be made strong with mindfulness. You have gained joy, happiness, and peace in jhana. These must be protected with mindfulness, without attachment to them. Only when you don't attach to joy, happiness, and peace can you fight Mara. Attachment is Mara's bait. If you swallow this bait, you lose the battle.

ATTAINING THE SECOND JHANA

The attainment of the second jhana does not take place by wishing or willing or striving. When the mind is ready to attain the second jhana, it automatically lets go of the first jhana. You don't even have to wish to go to the second jhana. When the mind is ready, it glides into the second jhana by itself. But only if you let it.

When you attained the first jhana, you let go of your many activities and all the hindrances that were such firm habits of mind. The second jhana is called "jhana without thought." To attain the second jhana you must let go of vitakka (applied thoughts of generosity, loving-friendliness, and compassion) and vicara (maintaining those thoughts with sustained application). Part of their function is to form words, to turn subtle thought into speech.

In meditation, especially in a retreat situation, we observe silence. We say that we observe "noble silence." In reality, as there are thoughts in the mind, our ordinary silence is not *real* noble silence. Word formation must totally stop to qualify our silence as "noble." The second jhana does not have discursive thought or sustained thought. Here your internal silence is truly noble. It is a genuine noble one's jhana. In this state, the mind really becomes calm.

The moment your thinking or subtle thoughts vanish from your mind, you are aware that you have entered the second jhana. But as soon as the thought, "This is the second jhana," appears in your mind, you lose it. Try again and again until that thought does not appear. You can stay with the awareness of second jhanic experience without the concept "this is the second jhana." This is a very delicate balance. Only with full awareness can you maintain it.

Before attaining the first jhana you practiced mindfulness to attain it. In the first jhana you use mindfulness to maintain an unfluctuating level of the jhana. Mindfulness plays a very important role in the first jhana to prevent hindrances from entering. Whenever you lose mindfulness, you lose the first jhana. Your jhanic concentration is not very strong and you can lose it very quickly.

The second jhana is more stable. Altogether, the second jhana has numerous factors, including internal confidence. This was absent in the first jhana. By overcoming the hindrance of doubt, you developed a certain degree of confidence in the Buddha, Dhamma, and

Sangha and in ethical principles. When you attain the second jhana, that confidence becomes stronger. Due to the fact that you have already experienced the first jhana, you experience even deeper confidence in your attainment and in the Buddha, Dhamma, and Sangha. You are making progress. You see that for yourself and it is beyond all possibility of doubt. Your upward path is very clear.

The second jhana also has a deeper level of concentration. You do not have to watch out for hindrances. The first jhana is still close to the hindrances and to all material experiences. The second jhana is still close to vitakka and vicara, but remote from hindrances. You should always be mindful of the possibility of losing the jhana. This is why you have cultivated mindfulness from the beginning.

> *With the subsiding of applied thought and sustained thought*
> *one enters and dwells in the second jhana,*
> *which has internal confidence and unification of mind,*
> *is without applied thought and sustained thought,*
> *and is filled with rapture and bliss born of concentration.*

As vitakka and vicara drop out of the picture, rapture, happiness, and one-pointedness remain. When thought drops away, you experience your entire body and mind filled with joy and happiness. This joy continuously replenishes itself with more and more joy. It is like a lake that has a spring underneath, continuously flowing with fresh water. From time to time it is cleansed by a very light rain shower that washes away whatever little dirt may fall upon the surface. Your mind is continuously refreshed and cleansed with new joy. It is constant and springing ever anew.

Attaining the Third Jhana

Now you are approaching the third jhana. Without wishing, the mind loses interest in the lower jhana and moves into the higher one. Joy is fading away. You don't do anything to make it fade. It does that naturally, by itself. This happens for two reasons. The first is that the mind loses interest in the second jhana. The second reason is that joy is affected by time and becomes impermanent.

You clearly experience the impermanence of the jhanic factors. That experience takes place while in jhana, as you are coming out of jhana, and when you reflect on the factors afterward. You don't have to spend any great deal of time to see the impermanence of the jhanic factors. The mindfulness you have cultivated does it.

In the preliminary stage, before attaining jhana, you had to make a strenuous effort to stay with the practice of moral principles. You disciplined yourself using the fourfold effort you learned in chapter 3; you learned to pick up good habits and drop bad ones. The mind was like a wild animal. It experienced the mundane enjoyment of sensual pleasures. Greed, hatred, delusion, and all the minor defilements were very strong. You needed a great deal of effort to overcome them, cultivate wholesome mental states, and maintain them. You have passed that stage. Holding off the defilements during meditation is much easier now.

Mindfulness and concentration united in the first jhana and were struggling to appear clearly. In the second jhana they became stronger, but still did not have enough strength to come out fully. In the third jhana they emerge completely and join hands. You can see them very clearly in the third jhana formula.

With the fading away of rapture,
one dwells in equanimity, mindful and discerning;

and one experiences in one's own person
that bliss of which the noble ones say:
"Happily lives one who is equanimous and mindful";
thus one enters and dwells in the third jhana.

The third jhana and fourth jhana are called "concentration without joy." Happiness (sukha) predominates, replacing the joy (piti) that has faded. When you are mastering the second jhana your mind keeps losing interest because of the coarseness of joy. It becomes more and more interested in the happiness, concentration, mindfulness, clear comprehension, and equanimity that begin to show up. When the mind completely loses interest in joy, it glides into the third jhana without your wishing or thinking. When the conditions for attaining the third jhana are present, mind itself chooses to move into it.

The third jhana has thirty-one factors. The joy drops away. It is seen to be coarse in comparison with the more refined happiness of the third jhana. The joy of the second jhana is like getting something. The happiness of the third jhana is like taking pleasure in it afterward. It is smoother, more unperturbed than joy.

When you attained the second jhana you experienced a very strong confidence from your success. As you are going through the practice of mastering the second jhana, your mind notices that the joy is getting weaker. Its opposite hindrance, restlessness and worry, is still haunting the mind from time to time. Each time you attain the second jhana your mind loses a bit of interest in joy. The mindfulness that you have practiced, even at the preliminary stage, before attaining the first jhana, is emerging, getting stronger.

You developed mindfulness and clear comprehension in the preliminary stage. They were present in the first jhana and second jhanas, too. Since the other factors in those jhanas were grossly dominating the mind, they did not come to prominence. Equanimity and clear comprehension also emerge in the third jhana. Now that the other jhanic factors have become weak, equanimity, mindfulness, and clear comprehension emerge to polish the third jhana.

MASTERY OF JHANA

You should not rush on to attain any higher jhana without thoroughly mastering the lower ones. You put your attention on fully mastering the first jhana before you attempt to attain the second. When you attain the first jhana many times, the mind loses interest in it because the shadow of thought is still lurking in the background.

It is a bit like the boredom you know in normal consciousness. Suppose you were struggling to obtain something you like very much. One day you get it. When you enjoy it for the first time, it is really wonderful. It is very tempting. You just love it. But as you go on enjoying it repeatedly for a long time, you lose interest in it. The pleasure you derive from that object or relationship gradually begins to diminish. Eventually the mind does not pay any attention to the object. It becomes just another thing you have, part of the backdrop of your life. The mind turns toward something else.

Similarly, you have been delighted with the subtle thoughts of renunciation, loving-friendliness, and non-cruelty that pervade the first jhana. After attaining the first jhana several times, you lose interest in these thoughts. Suppose you have attained the first jhana ten times. Each time, interest in these thoughts wears out a little. On the eleventh occasion, the mind may drop them completely. (Pay no attention to the numbers. It is just an example. You will work through the jhanas at your own pace.)

This means that, when the mind loses interest in the first jhana and is ready to drop it completely, you don't have to make any volitional effort to move on to the second jhana. It just happens. It happens in the same sequential order for everyone. When the preparatory state is well established, what comes next will simply happen—naturally. That is the nature of Dhamma.

Then your mind naturally goes to the second jhana. Confidence is strong in the second jhana because you have seen the result of the first jhana. After attaining the second jhana many times, you find it not giving you that same joy and happiness born of concentration that you experienced at the beginning of the second jhana. After attaining it many times, the same thing that happened in the first jhana happens in the second jhana. Joy becomes stale. Can you really turn away from a state of joy? Yes. The joy of jhana is not excitement as we know it in ordinary consciousness, but it is still a bit keyed up when compared with other, more refined states of mind. Restlessness can haunt you so long as joy is there. The mind loses interest in joy, which is dominant in the second jhana. Then the mind glides into the third jhana, where a more refined state of happiness is dominant.

THE STEPS OF MASTERY

How do you accomplish this "mastery" we speak of? Does it come all at once? No. Like many other things, there are natural steps in the process:

Step 1: Adverting. "Advert" means to turn the attention to something. Adverting, in this case, is the ability to bring your attention mindfully to the jhanic factors one by one after emerging from jhana.

That period right after your meditation session is very fruitful. Do not let this important opportunity pass you by. You should reflect on your jhana, especially when it has become stable, when you can attain it wherever you want, whenever you want, and for as long as you want. Then you can see it clearly.

Remember, the hindrances are not dead, just restrained. As any of these restrained hindrances becomes strong, you lose the jhana. You should find out which impediment has disturbed your jhana. Repeat the steps you followed to overcome that particular impediment. After it is once again subdued, you re-attain the jhana.

Step 2: Attaining. "Attaining" is your ability to enter jhana quickly. It improves with practice. Since you have already attained it, even though you lost it, you can attain it again quickly. Do so as promptly as you can, in this sitting, or the next, or as soon as you can set up the proper conditions. Do not let your mind forget how to do it. Strike while the iron is hot.

Step 3: Resolving. "Resolving" is the ability to make a decision to remain in the jhana for exactly a predetermined length of time. You resolve or decide to spend a certain amount of time in jhana. This ability is weak in the lower jhanas and grows in the higher ones.

You cannot determine to stay too long in any jhana lower than the fourth. The hindrances are only weakly restrained and still haunt the mind. Then you lose jhana. You should resolve to re-attain the jhana and to remain there for a certain period of time. Your ability will not be perfect. You will lose it again.

You must then resolve to see what has gone wrong. You find the reason. It is always one of the mental impurities that has snuck into your mind. Once you have found the particular hindrance that is causing the trouble, resolve to prevent it from arising again. Decide to overcome that particular impurity and to cultivate the wholesome state that supports the jhana. Be determined to maintain that wholesome state again.

This is the function of mindfulness in jhana. You apply mindfulness outside the jhana to find out the problem. You apply mindfulness within the jhana to maintain the state that preserves the jhana. So, with mindfulness you can overcome these impurities and with mindfulness you can re-attain and preserve the jhana.

Step 4: Emerging. "Emerging" means that you come out of the jhana without difficulty exactly at the predetermined time. You don't wait in jhana until you lose it. Here you attain jhana at will and come out of jhana at will. This is part of mastery.

Step 5: Reviewing. "Reviewing" means the ability to review the jhana and its factors with retrospective knowledge immediately after adverting to them. You have noticed the factor. Now you consciously review it. What you want to review is your progress on the path, how this jhanic experience has helped you. You review how you obtained jhana and what its benefits are. You consider how it has helped you overcome your own defilements and what defilements remain to be handled.

BEING IN JHANA

Why do you have to do all this after attaining a jhana? Jhana is like a juggling act. You keep things suspended in the air or balanced. Then you drop them. Then you start over. It takes a lot of practice and you need to figure out why you dropped the balls.

Being in jhana is like juggling five balls at once. They are the five jhanic factors. You are holding them all in the air without letting any of them fall to the ground. If one falls, they all fall. You must pick them up and start juggling all over again. What would make a ball fall? You are distracted—by fatigue, on-lookers, vehicles, sounds, or even by the joy of jhana.

While you are in jhana, a hindrance will appear in your mind. Maybe your body is hurting so much that your attention goes there. Maybe you hear a loud noise. Maybe you want lunch. Then you lose your jhana. You must start it all over again. Fortunately, you don't have to start from scratch because you have already learned to restrain hindrances. Simply go through these five steps of mastery and attain jhana again.

Have you ever seen a seal suspending a big ball in the air on its nose? He can hold it for a while. Then it falls to the ground. Then his trainer must pick it up and give it to him to do the same thing. Similarly, you can hold your concentration for a while. As soon as something disturbs your mind, you lose it. Then you pick it up again. Do not fret. You are learning, just like the seal.

Have you ever seen a balloon being suspended in the air for hours or days by a tube blowing air? That is a juggling act too. Once you manage to restrain the hindrances by balancing all the jhana factors, your concentration stays with you for a long time. You are learning this juggling act called jhana.

CHAPTER 12

The Fourth Jhana

If you continue refining your mindfulness, you can end up in the highest material jhana—the fourth. Here, mindfulness and equanimity are purified and come to a new level. Mindfulness acts as a shepherd for equanimity and keeps it in superb balance. The mind is pure, white, without stain, free from idiosyncrasies. It is soft, pliable, steady, and imperturbable.

All unsteady minds are upset by the thought of selflessness and suffering. Those minds are subject to an unpleasant emotional reaction when they investigate suffering. A foundation of well-developed equanimity corrects that. Unsteady minds want to experience only happiness, even though happiness never comes without suffering. It's like a buy-one-get-one-free deal. You get the second one, whether you want it or not. But when you are in the fourth jhana, steeped in extremely powerful and pure mindfulness and equanimity, your mind will not react emotionally to the words "suffering," "selflessness," and "impermanence" or to seeing the real things directly.

In the fourth jhana, nonverbal, non-conceptual realization begins to take place on a regular basis. The broad base of the eight steps of the Noble Eightfold Path gradually narrows down to the last step, concentration. The factors of enlightenment come together. Endowed with this powerful concentration, the fourth jhana penetrates the five aggregates and sees their impermanence, unsatisfactoriness, and selflessness at a nearly subatomic level. This is not inferential or theoretical knowledge. It is nonverbal, non-conceptual, and experiential, a direct seeing of the intrinsic nature of the aggregates.

Similarly, when you direct such an extremely powerful, clear mind toward the Four Noble Truths, your understanding becomes completely clear. The Four Noble Truths that you realize at this level are not gross in nature. They are the finest level of the Four Noble Truths. Jhana gradually gathers the force, power, and strength of concentration, to crack open the long-established shell of ignorance and get the full vision of liberation.

In this state verbal communication has totally ceased. The pure concentrated mind with pure mindfulness and equanimity clearly comprehends things without the sound of words or the vibration of thoughts. This is not the verbalizing or thinking stage. You already passed that long ago during your rational thinking phase. There you practiced the investigation factor of enlightenment in a verbal way, a way that took place before your mind became concentrated.

In the fourth jhana, you don't think conceptually about suffering, the cause of suffering, the end of suffering, or any of the rest. You just know, directly. This is the level where the mind sees things through the eye of wisdom. Words, thinking, investigation, or even reflection have no place. They would just get in the way. They are too slow and everything is moving too fast. Every cell in the body undergoes change every moment. When body changes at this inconceivable rapidity, no mind without powerful concentration can keep up. You need steadiness, pliability, softness, and purity to notice that flashing, incessant change. This sharpness of the mind is present only in the concentrated mind.

You must use this sharpness. You must focus your mindful attention on form, feeling, perception, thoughts, and consciousness so deeply that they disappear as discrete units. There is a single field, a range of form, feeling, perception, volitional formations, and consciousness. All that activity is happening within that range. Whatever notions you have had of "I" or "mine" or "I am" vanish. There is no "I" doing any of it.

JOINING BOTH

In the fourth jhana, concentrated mind penetrates the veil of pleasantness, pleasure, permanence, and self more clearly than ever before. It sees displeasure, suffering, impermanence, and non-self, craving, conceit, and wrong view more clearly. Tranquility and insight shake hands. This state is called "joining both."

In Brazil there is a thrilling sight. The River Solimoes and River Negro are two tributaries of the Amazon. These two giant rivers join at Manaus to make the Amazon River. The water in the two is different in color and they flow side by side for nearly six kilometers before they mix. I have seen this for myself on one of my teaching trips to Brazil. Mindfulness and concentration work that way in the fourth jhana. They blend together to form one mighty river.

You do not abandon this jhana. You don't let it subside. You don't overcome it as you did with the previous jhanas. You use it. You have been working very hard to attain this. It is not to be let go of like other jhanas, always passing on to something higher. You use it for developing insight.

The defilements you eradicate at this level are deeply settled in the mind. Only this kind of nonverbal, non-conceptual mindfulness with clear comprehension and equanimity can reach the very root of those deeply embedded defects. You simply direct attention onto your own underlying tendencies. Jhana opens the door. Working together, mindfulness and concentration weaken the fetters, so that later, in the supramundane jhanas, you can destroy them altogether.

Attaining the fourth jhana is called "Purification of Mind." From this purification wisdom arises.

> *With the abandoning of pleasure and pain,*
> *and with the previous disappearance of joy and grief,*
> *one enters and dwells in the fourth jhana,*
> *which has neither-pain-nor-pleasure*
> *and has purity of mindfulness and equanimity.*

Once you have attained the fourth jhana, you will not feel any need to come out of it. Equanimity predominates and you have strong "neither pleasant nor unpleasant" feelings. You stay as long as you have planned to stay. The world cannot disturb you. Pleasure and pain are abandoned. This "neutral feeling" is something that will persist throughout all the jhanas above the fourth.

In addition to the qualities that we have already mentioned, there are many mental factors in the fourth jhana (though six of them are repetitions from earlier jhanas). Once you have attained and mastered the fourth jhana, you can re-attain it any time without any problem.

COMING OUT OF JHANA TO PRACTICE VIPASSANA

Many people teach that we must come out of jhana to practice vipassana. Is that true?

The real question is, "Can your jhanic concentration penetrate things as they really are?" If the answer is "No," then your concentration is the absorption variety we spoke of earlier. It may well be wrong jhana. If the answer is "Yes," then your concentration is not absorption. It is right jhana.

According to the Buddha's teaching, when the mind is concentrated, you can see things as they really are. If your concentration is absorption without mindfulness, then you *should* come out of it because you are in wrong jhana. However, you *can* see things while you are in right jhana, and those things bear the stamp of the triple marks of all experience. They show anicca, dukkha, and anatta, which is what you are looking for and the reason you're doing all of this. So why should you come out of it to see things as they really are?

When we read about the way that the Buddha used his own fourth jhanic concentration, as given in many suttas, we have no reason to believe that he came out of jhana to develop the three kinds of knowledge that he used for seeing past lives, seeing beings dying and taking rebirth, and knowing that his own defilements had been destroyed.

If you can see things as they truly are when you are in access concentration, there is no reason to come out of it to practice vipassana. You are already achieving the goal of the practice. But, if you can see things as they actually are in access concentration, then you should be able to see things even better when you are in full right jhana, which is clearer and stronger than access concentration.

Should you come out of jhana and reflect upon the jhanic factors in order to understand the impermanence, suffering, and selflessness of jhanic factors themselves? It is virtually impossible to find evidence in the suttas that one should come out of jhana to practice vipassana. If you come out of jhana to practice vipassana, you lose the jhanic qualities because your hindrances return. The jhanic state is a perfect state of mind to focus on the Four Noble Truths, impermanence, unsatisfactoriness, and selflessness and to attain liberation by eliminating the fetters.

EQUANIMITY BASED ON DIVERSITY

Equanimity is the hallmark of the fourth jhana. Equanimity is a most altruistically balanced state of mind. A meditator in this state of mind is called "One who is living happily here and now." Happiness here is synonymous with peace and bliss.

A mind that grabs on to things constantly is constantly swept away, distracted. It cannot stay steady and uninvolved. It cannot simply see what is there. Equanimity releases you from this distraction. It is the dominant factor in the fourth jhana and it is the reason that the jhana can yield deep wisdom.

The equanimity that is sometimes present in normal consciousness depends on diversity, dividing conscious attention into apparently enduring "things." In vipassana meditation, you stay in the realm of diversity. You are still in touch with your senses. When you practice well, as each thing arises in the mind, you spot it and you pull yourself back to equanimity. Your equanimity is very rapid but not quite instantaneous. Each sensory experience arises and passes away in a flash. The mind does not hold on to it. Yet there is a measurable moment of its arising.

When we get immersed in the pleasantness or unpleasantness of a sensory object, we fail to notice its impermanence. The function of equanimity is to break this attachment reaction and reveal the impermanence of everything we experience in samsara.

Equanimity based on diversity can be explained with regard to six senses (including consciousness) and the objects of the six senses.

The eye and forms. When you see a form with your eyes, you begin to grasp on to it. Then you rapidly pull back into equanimity. If it was pleasant, you forget the pleasantness and register it as just a visual phenomenon. You use your equanimity to see the impermanence of what you saw.

The ear and sounds. When you hear a sound with the ear, you pull back to equanimity very quickly. If it was an unpleasant sound, you just drop the unpleasantness. It is simply a sound. You use your equanimity to see the impermanence of what you heard.

The nose and odors. When you smell an odor with the nose, you rapidly establish equanimity. You register it as simply an odor, neither pleasant nor unpleasant. You use your equanimity to see its impermanence.

The tongue and flavors. When you taste a flavor with the tongue, it is regarded as simply a flavor. You drop the wonderfulness or the horribleness or the neutrality. You see its impermanence.

The body and tangibles. When you touch a tangible with the body, you just register it as a touch. You establish your state of non-preference swiftly. You see the impermanence.

The mind and mind-objects. When you recognize a mind-object with the mind, you let it be just something held in the mind, neither good nor bad. You let it be just a mental phenomenon, inherently impermanent.

When you have "equanimity based on diversity," you spot and pull back from every sensory thing that arises in your perceptual world. When you do this well and consistently you are doing a good job at what is called "guarding your senses."

All this starts with mindfulness, of course. All the seven factors of Enlightenment begin with mindfulness. Your mindfulness must be sharp enough that you quickly notice yourself becoming involved in these perceptions. Only then can you establish the equanimity you need to drop the near-instantaneous reaction that follows.

EQUANIMITY BASED ON UNITY

A different sort of equanimity develops in the fourth jhana, where consciousness is unified by concentration. In the fourth jhana and beyond, sensory impressions do not arise at all. Your equanimity is not based on any of the six senses. It arises based purely on concentration or one-pointedness of mind, along with mindfulness. There is no room for sensory experience and thus equanimity is smooth and continuous. It takes no time because it is uninterrupted. When mindfulness is present, awareness of impermanence is smooth and steady.

The perfection of equanimity allows all the other factors to unite. This is where the factors of enlightenment you have been cultivating all come together. All the wholesome things you have been doing in your daily life—little by little, here and there—consolidate and produce results in the fourth jhana. When the fourth jhana is attained, its equanimity is based on this unity of mind. The mind is well unified in the second jhana. It becomes perfectly unified in the fourth jhana because your senses are not responding to sensory stimuli.

When you see impermanence in ordinary consciousness, it can be quite distressing. Everything is slipping away, all the time. You are attached to it and you want it to last. All the things you love are being lost or will be lost. You have strong emotional reactions to this. That is natural. However, in the fourth jhana, there are no emotional reactions. Equanimity and mindfulness are strong and clear. They become equal partners. You see impermanence, suffering, and selflessness, smoothly, without response. It just is as it is.

LIGHT AND VISION

At the very beginning of this book we said that the mind is luminous. Jhana is where you see that clearly. The mind is filled with a beautiful light. You see everything clearly.

When you attain the fourth jhana, this luminosity becomes prominent. Speaking of this luminous mind, the Buddha says:

> It has become malleable, wieldy, purified,
> bright, unblemished, and rid of defilement.
> It is steady and attained to imperturbability.

Luminosity is not explicitly stated in this formula but it is implied by purity, brightness, unblemished state, and a state free from defilement. This luminosity is very powerful. The Buddha used it to develop supernormal powers. Seeing previous lives and beings dying and taking rebirth are mundane supernormal powers. More significant is the kind of knowledge that can see the Four Noble Truths and destroy the defilements.

In jhana there is also an experience similar to visual light but not a product of the ordinary material senses. So long as a meditator is in right jhana, there is both light and vision. That is the state where the mind is perfectly clear to see the truth as it really is. Effort, mindfulness, and concentration work as a team to open the wisdom-eye that allows you to understand all things as they really are. Luminous mind shines most brilliantly, making the brightest vision.

We humans put a lot of emphasis on vision. Mindfulness and clear comprehension are often expressed as "seeing." After attaining enlightenment the Buddha met people said to have very little dust in their eyes. One who has attained the stream-entry fruition state (eliminating the belief in the self) is known as "One who has entered the vision." *Seeing* the truth is heavily emphasized in the texts. When the Buddha attained enlightenment he said, "*Eye* arose in me."

You can see the truth only when the wisdom-eye is clear. The wisdom-eye temporarily removes confusion or dust. Ignorance, expressed as fetters, has confused your mind for a long time. When the fetters are removed from the mind, your wisdom-eye can see the truth of impermanence in all conditioned things.

Explaining his own attainment of jhana, the Buddha said that he gained light and vision and soon both of them disappeared. Having considered the reason for this disappearance, he found that one of the imperfections had arisen in his mind and his concentration had fallen away. When concentration was there, light and vision were there. When concentration fell away, he lost both light and vision. Then he restarted the practice with mindfulness until he once again gained concentration, vision, and light.

Even a very tiny speck of dust can distort the clarity of a great, powerful telescope. Then it cannot bring to human eyes its pristine clarity of images. Your heart, brain, and nervous system do not operate to their maximum capacity if there is a single iota of dirt in them. It is far more important for the mind that is dealing with spiritual matters to remain totally free. Otherwise it cannot even temporarily recall previous lives or see beings dying and taking rebirth according to their kammas, as the Buddha did. Above all, and most importantly, it cannot destroy all the defilements. This is not intellectual speculation. This is seeing with a pure, clean, well-concentrated mind.

Only in the state of the fourth jhana are equanimity, mindfulness, and one-pointed concentration powerful enough to perform these feats. Once you come out of the fourth jhana, or any jhana for that matter, the mind begins to weaken in its strength and power. The longer you are out of jhana, the weaker the power and strength of jhana become until the hindrances return in their full strength.

Then your mind is nearly as it was before attaining jhana. You have the residue of jhana, but not the full strength and power.

It is very much like when you climb a mountain. At the top you have a huge, wide vision of the surrounding countryside. The world looks vast from up there. So long as you are there you can see all the surrounding area as far as your eyesight and visibility goes. If you come down even one step, you lose that vision. It is not the same. The farther down you go, the narrower your vision.

Similarly, so long as you are in the fourth jhana, the clarity, purity, steadiness, stainlessness, whiteness, equanimity, and imperturbability of the mind remain. When you come out they become weak. Eventually they are lost.

SIGNLESSNESS, NON-STICKINESS, AND VOIDNESS

In spite your mastery of jhana, you lose jhana. This is because your jhanic attainments are impermanent. Everything, even your long-sought jhana, is impermanent! You realize that everything operates within the boundary of this all-pervading impermanence. What is lost is lost forever. It is totally gone. There is no sign left behind. This is an experience of *signlessness*. You can see this directly in jhana and conceptually in your review afterward.

The concentrated mind can penetrate impermanence at three levels—rising, peaking, and passing away. These are the three minor moments of each instant of impermanence in body, feelings, perceptions, volitional formations, and consciousness. They occur in your concentrated mind like mustard seeds dropping into a hot frying pan. Your experience breaks into tiny pieces with a popping sound. It is like a drop of water dropping into a hot pan. It shatters into tiny particles, and evaporates quickly, without leaving any sign behind. Although you have known that everything is impermanent, this is the first time you experience impermanence at this intensity, at its subtlest level.

Repeated loss of what you have gained is very frustrating. This is unsatisfactoriness or dukkha. Desire is the glue that sticks thoughts, ideas, feelings, and perceptions to the mind. You see with the eye of wisdom that this glue, affected by all-pervading impermanence, is drying, weakening. Its grip is slipping away. At this point, nothing sticks to the mind. This is called *non-stickiness*.

You realize that there is no way to keep your jhanic attainment. You will always lose it when you come out of jhana. This sense of loss deepens your frustration. What is this "you" that keeps gaining and losing a whole world of experience? It is not really there. There is just experience, rising and falling, coming and going. This is your insight into the reality of selflessness, anatta. You see void or vacuum in what has been lost. This is called *voidness*.

These insights, however, are not very deep. These experiences of signlessness, non-stickiness, and voidness are superficial. But they are very useful.

USING THE FOURTH JHANA

You pause at the fourth jhana rather than passing on to some higher state. You *use* the fourth jhana. There is no transition from the fourth jhana to any intermediary state. The qualities of the fourth jhana provide the mind its best opportunity for seeing the finest level of change in the five aggregates. The mind is pure, clear, and refined.

The Buddha was always mindful. His mind was always pure, clean, equanimous, imperturbable, bright, shining, and steady. Yet, still he attained the fourth jhana to get the sharpest and most powerful one-pointed concentration. Only when you are in the deepest level of meditation do you experience the minute level of the changes taking place in your mind and body. Words, thoughts, and concepts stop, but the feeling of impermanence goes on. This is where you perceive that the Dhamma is unaffected by time. This means that the element of Dhamma that the Buddha taught us is always present. You experience it only when you are mindful and concentrated in deep meditation.

You cannot put this experience into words. This is the state where the law of Dhamma is distinctly present in your mind. It is here that you see suffering, but you do not suffer from suffering. You can see the truth of all dhammas, all feelings, all consciousness, all thoughts, and all perceptions. The truth that you see in all of them is that they all are flowing through the awareness. They are just flowing through. Nothing is sticking. The attention does not snag on anything. It just flows.

You must go through rigorous training. It takes all the elements we have discussed to gain concentration of this quality—virtue, restraint, mindfulness, clear comprehension, contentment, making effort, choosing a secluded place, and metta practice. As you are not attached to these wholesome thoughts, in spite of the fact that they are very pleasing, you can stay mindfully in this state without coming out of it and without being attached to it. This is the state you protect without being attached to it.

Protecting what has been won,
clinging to nothing.

Your attention, mindfulness, and concentration work together to see the impermanence, unsatisfactoriness, and selflessness of these jhanic factors themselves, which are not thoughts but dynamic actions or activities in the mind and body. Mind can easily notice them as they occur. In fact, in jhana they are clearer and more prominent than at any other time.

Even after coming out of jhana, you remember the factors that were present in jhana. But then what you have experienced is all gone. Reflecting on the impermanence, unsatisfactoriness, and self-lessness of these factors is most effective while you are participating in them, not before or after.

You experience the impermanence of anything best while you are actually experiencing it. What you do after or before your experience is intellectualizing or philosophizing, using logic and reason.

Probably the most important of the ancient teachers of the past is Venerable Buddhaghosa. He created the great Theravada compendium called the *Visuddhimagga*, or *Path to Purification*. One thing he pointed out is that one meaning of jhana is to burn up the factors opposing jhana. You cannot burn them by thinking about them. You burn anything when the objects are there, actually present.

Defilements have "influxes" and "outfluxes." They flow into the mind and brew there, becoming ever more potent. Then they flow out with even more force. They manifest as harsh words and evil deeds and emotional uproar. In jhana, you burn these influxes and outfluxes directly. They are deep down in your subconscious mind, but they are coming up to the conscious level in small, subtle doses during jhana.

The jhanic state is very calm, peaceful, and quiet. Your concentration, with mindfulness and equanimity purified, can reach these influxes and outfluxes and uproot them. It is not impeded by emotional reaction. If you try to do this outside jhana, you will be simply trying to use your logical, rational thinking to eliminate them. It will not be successful. You can burn or eliminate them in a deep, concentrated state of mind. That is the time the mind is fully qualified to eradicate them. For defilements to burn, they must arise in the mind. They must be burnt as they are arising, neither before nor after.

Jhana can help you burn the ill influences out of the mind in other ways too. Sometimes, while listening to the Dhamma, your mind can go into deep concentration. You can see the meaning of the Dhamma, see the meaning of life, and remove the roots of greed, hatred, and delusion while sitting right there on that very same spot. That is why, when the Buddha gave Dhamma talks, many people— monks, nuns, men, and women—attained stages of enlightenment. These mental states become crystal clear when the mind is free from hindrances and other psychic irritants.

You might even remember something like this. It happens to everyone. While listening to a talk, you lose the thread. For a while, your mind is not on the talk. It is somewhere else, deeply engaged in something else. After some time your mind returns. During the time your mind was thinking of something else you did not even hear the speaker.

The same mental process can take place while listening to a Dhamma talk. While the speaker is giving the Dhamma talk, your mind goes into the deep meaning of the words he utters. Then you see the intrinsic nature of the things the speaker says. The Dhamma becomes perfectly clear. You realize the perfection of the Buddha's teaching through a little window of vision into the clarity and purity of Dhamma. As this realization arises, your mind experiences the pristine purity of Dhamma and your doubt vanishes.

At this moment you enter the path of "stream entry."

CHAPTER 13

The Immaterial Jhanas

You do not need the immaterial jhanas to achieve liberation. What is essential is the practice of the Noble Eightfold Path. However, the practice of the immaterial jhanas can contribute to the growth of calm and insight. They can embellish the spiritual perfection of a meditator, so the Buddha included them in his discipline. They are options for you if you are inclined to develop them.

THE FOUR ARUPPAS

The four immaterial jhanas are called the *aruppas* or "peaceful immaterial liberations transcending material form." They are not designated by numerical names like their predecessors, but by the names of their objective spheres: the base of boundless space; the base of boundless consciousness; the base of voidness; the base of neither perception nor non-perception.

They are called "formless" or "immaterial" for two reasons: First, they are achieved by overcoming all perceptions of material form (*rupa*), even of the subtle material form of the counterpart sign of your meditation object. And second, they are the subjective counterparts of the immaterial planes of existence.

The movement from any lower jhana to its successor involves the elimination of the coarser jhanic factors. The refinement of

consciousness that occurs hinges upon actual changes in the com-
position of the states. However, when you ascend from the fourth
jhana to the first immaterial jhana, and from one immaterial jhana
to another, there are no changes in these compositional factors. The
fourth jhana and all four formless jhana attainments have precisely
the same factors of consciousness. The factors in each higher attainment are subtler than those in its predecessors, more peaceful and
more sublime, but they do not differ in number or in their essential
nature.

You achieve the climb from one formless attainment to another by
changing the object of concentration, not by eliminating or replacing component factors. All five states contain the same two jhanic
factors: one-pointedness and "neither painful nor pleasant" feeling.

The First Aruppa: The Base of Boundless Space

The four formless attainments must be achieved in sequence, beginning with the base of boundless space and culminating in the base
of neither perception nor non-perception. The motivation that leads
you to seek the immaterial states is a clear recognition of the dangers
posed by gross physical matter. You might also be repelled by matter
as a result of considering the numerous afflictions to which your
physical body is vulnerable. You can have eye diseases, ear diseases,
and all the other things that bodies are plagued with.

If you want to escape these dangers, you must first attain the four
material jhanas. You enter the fourth jhana, taking as your object
any of the kasinas except the limited space kasina. At that point you
have risen above gross matter, but you still have not completely tran-
scended all material form. The self-luminous counterpart sign, the
object of your jhana, is still a material form. To reach the formless
attainments you must genuinely yearn to rise completely above the

materiality of the kasina. The countersign's materiality is the counterpart of gross matter. It shares the defects of matter.

Why should you be afraid of ordinary, physical matter? Buddhaghosa gives us a simile. Suppose a timid man is pursued by a snake in the forest. He flees. Later he sees something resembling the snake. It might be a palm leaf with a streak painted on it, a creeper, a rope, or a crack in the ground. He becomes fearful and anxious. He does not want to look at it.

You can be frightened by seeing the danger in gross matter, as the man was afraid of the snake. You can flee from gross matter and escape by reaching the fourth jhana. You can observe that the subtle matter of the kasina is the counterpart of gross matter and not want to look at it.

Once you have generated a strong desire to reach the immaterial jhanas, you must achieve the five steps of mastery of the fourth jhana you learned in chapter 11. Then, after emerging from the jhana, you perceive its defects and the benefits of the next higher attainment. The defects are:

The fourth jhana has an object of material form. It is still connected with gross matter.

It is close to happiness, a factor of the third jhana.

It is coarser than the immaterial attainments.

You then see the *base of boundless space* as more peaceful and sublime than the fourth jhana and as more safely removed from materiality. The method for attaining this first formless jhana is to extend the kasina mentally "to the limit of the world-sphere, or as far as you like." You then remove the kasina by attending exclusively to the space it covered.

The original physical kasina provides the preliminary sign for concentration. You keep focusing your mind on it until the mental image or learning sign appears. This memorized mental image is apprehended as clearly as the physical object. Concentration on the learning sign gives rise to the counterpart sign. This conceptualized image is used as the object for access concentration and the material jhanas.

After entering each jhana, you learn to extend the sign outward by degrees, making the visualized kasina cover increasingly larger areas—up to a world system or more. Now, to reach the base of boundless space, you must remove the kasina and attend exclusively to the space it has been made to cover.

> *When he is removing it,*
> *he neither folds it up like a mat*
> *nor withdraws it like a cake from a tin.*
> *It is simply that he does not advert to it*
> *or give attention to it or review it;*
> *it is when he neither adverts to it*
> *nor gives attention to it nor reviews it*
> *but gives his attention exclusively*
> *to the space touched by it*
> *[regarding that] as "space, space,"*
> *that he is said to "remove the kasina."*

Taking as your object the space left after the removal of the kasina, you advert to it as "boundless space, boundless space," or simply as "space, space." You strike at it with applied and sustained thought. You cultivate this practice again and again, repeatedly developing it until the concept reaches maturity. When your development is fully matured, a new moment of consciousness arises with boundless space as its object.

With the complete surmounting of perceptions of matter,
with the disappearance of perceptions of resistance,
with non-attention to perceptions of variety,
aware of "unbounded space,"
he enters into and dwells in
the base consisting of boundless space.

Several phrases in this formula may benefit from some clarification: "With the complete surmounting of perceptions of matter" means that you transcend all material perceptions, both the ordinary perception of the physical kasina and its subtle counterpart sign. You have left behind the mental objects you used to achieve and sustain the material jhanas.

"With the disappearance of the perceptions of resistance" means that every physical perception contains a striking of the sense organs upon some sensory object. There is always a slight resistance, a moment of felt impact. You also leave this behind.

"With non-attention to perceptions of variety" means that every time you experience any one thing, you are distinguishing that object from all other perceptions. You are chopping your experiential world into pieces. You leave this sense of diversity behind as well.

"Unbounded space" means that since there are no separate perceptions, no boundary for the space can be perceived. There can be no "beginning" or "middle" or "end." It is boundless.

What results are discrete moments of consciousness, with discrete names in the Pali language. There are three or four moments of access concentration, still in touch with the physical senses and characterized by equanimity. Then follows the moment of complete engagement in the subtle feeling of boundless space.

A note relative to the limited space kasina—There's a small tricky point here. You can use any of the kasinas except the limited space kasina, which is meant to stand for any restricted space. Meditators usually concentrate on a hole in a wall, the space inside a keyhole, a window—something like that. The objective of this exercise is to expand your meditation object until it fills and represents boundless space. You cannot expand limited space to boundless space. Limited means limited. This meditation object simply will not work for this exercise.

THE SECOND ARUPPA:
THE BASE OF BOUNDLESS CONSCIOUSNESS

To attain the second aruppa, you must achieve full mastery over the first and then see its defects. It is still close to the material jhanas and it is less peaceful than the attainments above it. You reflect on these defects until they are real to you. Then the mind naturally develops indifference toward the first aruppa and you turn your attention toward the second.

> *By completely surmounting the base*
> *consisting of boundless space,*
> *aware of "unbounded consciousness,"*
> *he enters and dwells in*
> *the base consisting of boundless consciousness.*

You focus upon the consciousness that is aware of that boundless space. This consciousness is also boundless and even more refined. You advert to it as "boundless consciousness" or simply as "awareness, awareness." Your object is awareness but you always keep that boundless, infinite nature in mind.

These are normal conscious thoughts and you turn to them again and again. You repeat to yourself over and over "awareness, awareness." The hindrances are restrained and the mind enters access concentration. You continue to cultivate the counterpart sign that results. There follows a moment of complete engagement in the "base of boundless consciousness."

THE THIRD ARUPPA:
THE BASE OF NOTHINGNESS (VOIDNESS)

To attain the next aruppa, the base of nothingness, you fully master the base of boundless consciousness. Then, after reviewing it, you become convinced that this attainment is imperfect due to its proximity to the base of boundless space. It is gross compared to the next higher jhana. By recognizing these defects, you remove your attachment. You perceive that the base of nothingness is more peaceful. The formula is:

> By completely surmounting
> the base consisting of boundless consciousness,
> aware that "there is nothing,"
> he enters upon and dwells in
> the base consisting of nothingness.

To concentrate on the base of nothingness, you give attention to the non-existence, the voidness, and the secluded aspect of the base of boundless space. The consciousness of boundless space was an experience. It is gone. It is no longer present in your mind. You attend to that absence. The boundless space contained nothing. That too is absence. You attend to that absence.

The *Visuddhimagga* explains it this way: A monk sees a group of monks assembled in a hall. Then he goes away. When he returns they are gone. He does not think about the monks or where they have gone. He just concentrates on their current absence, the total vacancy of the hall.

You advert to this absence over and over. You think to yourself, "there is not, there is not" or "void, void," or "nothing, nothing." The hindrances are restrained. Access concentration ensues. You continue to attend to the subtle counterpart sign that replaces the conscious thoughts. When this practice matures, there arises a moment of full engagement, a consciousness "belonging to the base of nothingness."

The base of boundless consciousness and base of nothingness are both concerned with the consciousness of the base of boundless space. However, they relate to it in opposite ways. The second aruppa objectifies it positively, focusing upon its content, the consciousness or awareness that fills the infinite space. The third aruppa focuses on its lack of content.

The "base of boundless consciousness" that must be surmounted is both the second immaterial jhana and its object.

The Fourth Aruppa: The Base of Neither Perception nor Non-Perception

If you choose to go further and reach the fourth and final aruppa, you must first achieve the five steps of mastery over the base of nothingness. Then you contemplate the defectiveness of that attainment and the superiority of the base of neither perception nor non-perception. You can also reflect upon the inherent unsatisfactoriness of perception. You can think, "Perception is a disease. Perception is a boil. Perception is a dart. The state of neither perception nor non-perception is more peaceful. It is sublime." This ends your attachment to the third aruppa and arouses a desire to attain the next.

The fourth aruppa has as its object the four mental aggregates that constitute the attainment of the base of nothingness: feeling, perception, mental formations, and consciousness. The second aruppa took as its object the consciousness belonging to the first aruppa. Similarly, the fourth aruppa takes as its object the consciousness of the third aruppa and its associated states.

Focusing on these four mental aggregates of the base of nothingness, you advert to that state as "peaceful, peaceful." You review it, strike at it with vitakka, and sustain the thought with vicara. The hindrances are restrained. The mind enters access concentration. You then pass into total engagement in the base of neither perception nor non-perception.

> *By completely surmounting*
> *the base consisting of nothingness,*
> *he enters and dwells*
> *in the base*
> *consisting of neither perception nor non-perception.*

You attain the fourth aruppa by passing beyond the base of nothingness. Yet this fourth attainment has the third as its object. You reach the fourth aruppa by focusing upon the base of nothingness as "peaceful, peaceful."

How can you overcome the base of nothingness if you attend to it? The *Visuddhimagga* provides an answer. Although you attend to the third aruppa as peaceful, you have no desire to attain it. This is because you have already decided that the fourth aruppa is more peaceful and sublime.

Buddhaghosa gives the example of a king who sees craftsmen at work while proceeding along a city street. He admires their skill but does not want to become a craftsman himself. He is aware of the superior benefits of kingship.

The name "base of neither perception nor non-perception" suggests the abstruse nature of this jhana. On one hand, it lacks gross perception. On the other, it retains a certain subtle perception. Lacking gross perception, it cannot perform the decisive function of perception—the clear discernment of objects. Thus it cannot be said to have perception. Yet it retains an extremely subtle perception. Thus it cannot be said to be without perception. Perception, feeling, consciousness, contact, and the rest of the mental factors continue here, but are reduced to the finest subtlety. This jhana is also named the "attainment with residual formations."

The commentaries illustrate the meaning with the following anecdote. A novice smears a bowl with oil. An elder monk asks him to bring the bowl to serve gruel. The novice replies, "Venerable sir, there is oil in the bowl." The monk tells him, "Bring the oil, novice. I shall fill the oil tube." The novice says, "There is no oil, venerable sir."

What the novice said is true in both cases. There is "no oil" since there is not enough to fill the tube. Yet there is no utter absence of oil since some remains in the bowl.

With this fourth formless jhana, the mind has reached the highest possible level of development in the direction of serenity. Consciousness has attained the most intense degree of concentration. It has become so subtle and refined that it can no longer be described in terms of existence or non-existence. Yet even this attainment, as we will see, is still a mundane state. From the Buddhist perspective, it must finally give way to insight. Insight alone leads to true liberation. We cover these points in the final chapter.

CHAPTER 14

The Supramundane Jhanas

There are said to be four stages in the supramundane enlightenment process. They are: stream-enterer; once-returner; never-returner; arahant.

The stages occur in this order and we will lookw at each of them in this chapter. You attain the supramundane jhanas at the moment of stream entry.

Those who attain mundane jhanas restrain hindrances but don't destroy them. Mundane jhana attainers live happily so long as they do not lose their jhanic attainment. Those who attain the supramundane jhanas, on the other hand, destroy the hindrances as well as fetters.

Attainers of mundane jhana alone may still have the desire to "be reborn in the Brahma realms," which is to say, to gain some better circumstance than they have now. They may still have hopes for some future self, different from and better than their present situation. But supramundane jhana attainers destroy any desire whatsoever to be born in any form or shape. It is written that, if the meditator attains the supramundane jhanas without attaining full enlightenment, he will be reborn a limited number of times, and only in higher planes of existence.

The final step of the path is the wisdom of full liberation. Everybody who attains any stage of enlightenment attains that state in supramundane jhanic concentration. Attaining full enlightenment brings rebirth to an end completely.

THE SUPRAMUNDANE NOBLE PATH

The supramundane jhanas are also called the Supramundane Noble Path. You began your practice with the mundane Noble Eightfold Path. There was still some doubt in your mind. When you overcome doubt, you see the truth for yourself and enter the Supramundane Noble Eightfold Path. From that moment onward, until you attain full enlightenment, you are following the supramundane level of the Noble Eightfold Path.

Each of the factors of the Noble Eightfold Path has two aspects. The *mundane* aspect is "subject to the cankers, pertaining to the side of merit, and maturing in the foundation of existence." The *supramundane* aspect is, "noble, free from cankers, supramundane, and a factor of the path."

Even at the mundane level of the path, you have to develop right view, right resolve, right speech, right action, right livelihood, right effort, and right mindfulness to attain right concentration. Now each must be developed fully, all the way to the supramundane level. Supramundane unification of mind is a noble, stainless state that abolishes any unwholesome mental condition.

Progress on the Noble Eightfold Path can be roughly divided into four phases. Each corresponds to a person's level of jhanic attainment: *Uninstructed worldlings* are blocked by hindrances and fetters. They generally have no personal acquaintance with jhana.

Instructed worldlings have entered the mundane path. If they employ jhana at all, it is the mundane jhanas, in which hindrances are held at bay but not removed from the mind.

Noble Disciples have crossed over into the Supramundane Noble

Path. They employ the supramundane jhanas to eradicate the fetters that hold hindrances in place and bind them into samsara.

Arahants have no further work to do. The fetters are gone and they use the jhanas for "pleasant abiding."

All the steps of the Noble Eightfold Path are mental states. That is true of both the mundane and the supramundane expressions of the path. When you see deeply, as a real experience, with your own wisdom-eye, that all conditioned things are impermanent, your mind state changes. Your superficial understanding of impermanence becomes a deep understanding and you attain the stream-entry path. From that point onward, the Noble Eightfold Path becomes the Supramundane Noble Path and you start demolishing the bridges that connect this life with the next.

Destroying Doubt

To attain stream entry, you must overcome doubt, which is classified as both a hindrance and a fetter. When you attain the mundane jhanas, you restrain doubt, but when you attain stream entry, you destroy it. It is easier to destroy doubt if you have weakened it. You learned to sidestep doubt in order to enter jhana. That made it weak enough that you can subject it to the intense scrutiny of mindfulness and burn it up forever.

There are two personality types who have less trouble with doubt: The first type, the *faith-follower*, is a person whose primary vehicle for the attainment of enlightenment is faith. He follows a devotional path based on deep faith in the Buddha, Dhamma, and Sangha. Due to this strong faith, he can attain the stream-entry path without attaining any mundane jhana. His faith allows him to destroy doubt.

The second type, the *Dhamma-follower* or *Wisdom-follower*, is a person whose primary vehicle on the path is a deep understanding of the Dhamma. He uses the intellect extensively. His reason leads him to the deep, wordless understanding that is true wisdom. He can attain the stream-entry path through penetrative insight alone, without attaining jhana. His insight allows him to destroy doubt.

Only these personality types can go directly to the supramundane jhanas to destroy the fetters. Others need the mundane jhanas to weaken them first.

So are you either of these types? Be honest. What happens to the rest of us? Do we still have a chance for liberation? The answer is a resounding, "Yes!" And this is precisely what jhanas are for.

STAGES OF THE SUPRAMUNDANE NOBLE PATH

Each of the four stages of the Supramundane Noble Path is divided into a path phase and a fruition phase. Both phases have definite characteristics. For each stage, there is a specific realization that marks the beginning of the path phase and another that signals "graduation" to the fruition phase. Each stage is marked by the elimination of one or more of the fetters. The order in which these are destroyed depends on your personality type. Faith-followers destroy the fetters in one order. Dhamma-followers proceed by another sequence.

The Abhidhamma Pitaka is an ancient work that provides a detailed analysis of the principles that govern mental and physical processes. It is a detailed scholastic reworking of doctrinal material appearing in the suttas, according to schematic classifications and numerous lists.

In the Abhidhamma texts, there is some suggestion that the path and the fruition periods can arise very rapidly, almost simultaneously. I feel that each phase may take a moment, a lifetime, or anywhere in between. The texts say that reflection on what is being accomplished at each stage of the process is very important, and there must be time for this reflection to take place. In addition, some texts talk about the comparative amount of merit obtained from offering gifts to someone who is in one or another of these stages. To me this means that people remain in each stage long enough to be distinguished from one another.

Other suttas imply that the path phase arises first. Then the meditator associates with the path phase, develops it, and cultivates it before attaining the fruition state. This means that the person has time to associate, cultivate, and develop the path before attaining the fruition state. Even if somebody's attainment seems instant, he still must attain the path first and afterward attain fruition. Attaining path and fruition at once is impossible. It is never mentioned in any sutta.

When you practice the Supramundane Noble Path, you become one of the "eight noble disciples of the Buddha." A "noble disciple" is one who enters the Noble Eightfold Path at the supramundane level. This is the stage at which "his fetters fade away." Such a person has already attained at least stream entry with concentration at the supramundane jhanic level.

In each phase of each stage, it is important to reflect on the process. The ancient texts lay out four things to reflect on: what defilements have been destroyed, which ones remain to be handled, the path that led to that destruction, the fruition that resulted.

Stream Entry

The first supramundane jhana destroys the first three fetters: belief in a permanent self, doubt, and attachment to rites and rituals. The precise order in which these three fetters are eliminated depends on your personality. If your path is faith, then at the attainment of the stream-entry path you will first destroy doubt. If your path is wisdom, then at the attainment of the stream-entry path you will first destroy the notion of self. The description below follows the first of these options.

Path. At the path phase of stream entry, you "attain the Dhamma, understand the Dhamma, and fathom the Dhamma." You cross beyond doubt, do away with perplexity, gain intrepidity, and establish yourself in the Buddha's teaching without depending on others. Up until now your doubt has been held at bay by the joy of the second jhana. This is the level at which you experience the complete disappearance of doubt. No sign remains of your previous confusion concerning the Buddha, Dhamma, Sangha, and morality.

You go on practicing the Noble Eightfold Path at the supramundane level. Your belief in attaining liberation by following rites and rituals disappears without a trace. You realize that no ritual that you have been following in the past could bring you the knowledge you have gained. Only the practice of Dhamma and the gaining of right concentration have done that.

Fruition. You attain stream-entry fruition when you overcome the belief in a separate self. There is still a lingering sense of "I" in the mind, but you don't take it seriously.

This awareness arouses your firm confidence in the Buddha, Dhamma, and Sangha, the noble disciples who became noble by following the Buddha and his teaching. You now have full confidence that there is life before this life, and that there are beings who have followed his path and attained full liberation from suffering.

With confidence, the strength of your faith, and the clear understanding that there is no self, you proceed. You pay attention to the impermanent nature of your bodily and mental experiences. You remember that all your past physical and mental experiences have changed. Similarly, all physical and mental experiences of the future will change, too. All past, present, and future experiences arise and pass away. You understand that the five aggregates, form, feeling, perceptions, thoughts, and consciousness, are all of the same nature, arising and passing away. They are all due to causes and conditions. When those conditions change, they pass away.

Knowing that there is birth before and after death, fear arises. You realize that if you don't liberate yourself from suffering immediately, you will be reborn. You will suffer through the same pain, sorrow, grief, and despair. You may fear that you will die without liberating yourself from all this suffering. Knowing this, you wish to liberate yourself from samsara altogether. You want never to be born again.

Once-Returner

The second supramundane jhana weakens your addiction to sensual pleasure and hatred.

Path. Now you see the five aggregates constantly, every single tiny event, in every single breath. You notice that every intentional occurrence in your body and mind involves all five aggregates. As they involve themselves in each and every thing you intentionally do, you see their tiny little parts in a constant state of flux. They change without remaining the same for even a fraction of a second. When the gross part of your lust vanishes you enter the once-returner's path.

Fruition. When the gross part of your hatred vanishes, you enter the once-returner's fruition stage.

If you have been a person prone to hate, the first fetter to be overcome is the gross part of lust. If you have been more prone to lust, you overcome the gross part of hatred first. Whichever fetter has been predominant will be the last to be overcome. Notice that we said "the gross part" of anger and desire. The subtle part of each remains.

Never-Returner

The third supramundane jhana destroys for good addiction to sensual pleasure and hatred. One meditator may first destroy greed for sensual pleasure. Another might destroy hatred first. This difference depends, as before, on the person's temperament and character.

Path. With more vigor, courage, confidence, and clarity than ever, you practice the Noble Eightfold Path at the supramundane level. When the loving-friendliness, compassion, appreciative joy, and equanimity that were initiated at the attainment of the first jhana come to fruition, the subtle level of hatred totally vanishes from your mind. At that moment, you enter the never-returner's path.

Fruition. Then, when the last remnant of craving for sensual pleasures vanishes forever, you enter the state of never-returner's fruition.

Arahant

The fourth supramundane jhana destroys the final five fetters: desire for material existence, desire for immaterial existence, conceit, restlessness, and ignorance. When you make the jump from mundane right concentration to supramundane right concentration, your luminous mind can be permanently purified from external defilements. The result is arahantship.

Path. Here all desire for material existence evaporates. As you progress on that path, desire for material and immaterial existence, conceit, and restlessness each vanish from your mind.

Fruition. Finally, the last residue of the I-maker, and the last iota of ignorance of the Four Noble Truths are erased from your mind. At that point, you attain the fruition of full enlightenment.

Then this thought arises: "Birth is exhausted, lived is the holy life, done is what was to be done, there is nothing more to be done."

At this point, you have attained liberation, the ultimate goal of Buddhist practice, through a long, arduous process of awakening.

And it all began with the simple observation of a breath going in and out.

Glossary

ABANDONING: Giving up unwholesome habits.

ABHIDHAMMA: The Abhidhamma is Theravada Buddhism's gigantic compendium of everything known about meditation and related subjects.

ABSORPTION: One way jhana is often translated is "absorption." It is not just any state of absorption. You can be absorbed in almost anything. Jhana is more. It is achieved by contemplating specific subjects and has specific qualities.

ACCESS CONCENTRATION: The transition point from non-jhana to jhana and is called access concentration. You can attain jhana only after overcoming hindrances. You battle and subdue the hindrances in the state of access concentration.

Concentration is still unsteady, but your mind keeps trying and it is getting easier. You fluctuate between your calm focus and your inner dialog. You are still open to your senses. You hear and feel in the normal way but it is off in the background. The breath is a dominant thought—an object, a thing—but it is not your only focus. Strong feelings of zest or delight set in. There is happiness, satisfaction, and a special state of non-preference called equanimity. They are very weak, but they begin to arise.

ADVERTING: To turn the mind or attention toward something. *Adverting*, among other meanings, is the ability to bring your attention mindfully to the jhanic factors one by one after emerging from jhana. This is part of jhana mastery.

ANATTA: *No-self*—The realization that neither "I" nor any other conditioned "thing" is actually self-existing in its essence. All apparent "things" are temporary collections of impermanent elements, undergoing continuous, sometimes subtle change.

ANICCA: *Impermanence*—The realization that all things arise and pass away and that their very nature is incessant change. Anicca is not just a word or concept. Anicca is real. It is the actual experience of what is really going on in our body and mind. It is all changing constantly. Our body, mind, and everything in our sensory world is changing constantly.

ARAHANT: The fourth stage of the supramundane path to enlightenment where all desire for material existence evaporates. The last residue of the I-maker, and the last iota of ignorance of the Four Noble Truths are also erased from your mind.

ATTAINING: This is your ability to enter jhana quickly. It improves with practice. This is part of jhana mastery.

AWARENESS: Having knowledge of (example: "He had no awareness of his mistakes"); state of elementary or undifferentiated consciousness (example: "The crash intruded on his awareness").

CLEAR COMPREHENSION: See Sampajanna

CONCENTRATION: Concentration is a gathering together of all the positive forces of the mind, tying them into a bundle, and welding them into a single intense beam that will stay where we point it.

COUNTERPART SIGN: The object of focus itself is called a "preliminary sign" or "learning sign." It means something used for learning. The meditator gazes at it until he or she memorizes it. The memorized picture is called the "counterpart sign." The meditator holds this counterpart sign in mind and uses it as the meditation object to enter jhana.

CRAVING: Desire to have more or less of something. The existence of objects in the world does not cause craving to arise in your mind automatically. But when you encounter them and reflect on them in an unwise manner, craving is the result.

Craving is one of the most powerful of the unwholesome roots, the deepest forces of the mind, the ones that feed the fetters. It is nourished by the injudicious consideration of these objects. The cause of suffering is craving. Once craving is eliminated, suffering will be eliminated.

DISCURSIVE THOUGHT: Discursive means "proceeding to a conclusion by reason or argument rather than intuition." In this book we divide "thought" into two categories. *Discursive thought* is the one-concept-leading-to-the-next variety of thought you hear most of the time, like a voice speaking in your head. *Subtle thought* is nonverbal and intuitive.

DOUBT: One of the five hindrances. Do you have to accept everything your teacher says on faith, without proof and without any analysis of your own? No. But certain doubts are deadly: *Emotional doubt* is doubt about the Buddha, the Sangha, and morality. *Intellectual doubt* is doubting essential aspects of the Dhamma.

DUKKHA: *Suffering, Unsatisfactoriness*—The realization that some amount of suffering exists in every experience within samsara.

EMERGING: This means that you come out of the jhana at will and without difficulty at a predetermined time. You don't wait in jhana until you lose it. You attain jhana at will and come out of jhana at will. This is part of jhana mastery.

FACTOR: A component or aspect of something. For example, there are thirty-seven factors of enlightenment and they are divided into seven overlapping groups.

They are the four foundations of mindfulness; the four bases for spiritual power; the four efforts; the five spiritual faculties; the five spiritual powers; the Noble Eightfold Path; the seven factors of enlightenment.

All these are called "factors." A separate group, the seven factors of awakening, subsumes and contains all the others.

FACTORS OF ENLIGHTENMENT OR FACTORS OF AWAKENING: See Thirty-seven Factors of Enlightenment

FAITH-FOLLOWER: Someone whose primary vehicle on the path is faith. Faith is his vehicle for the attainment of enlightenment. He follows a devotional path based on deep faith in the Triple Gem. If he has strong faith in the Triple Gem, he can attain the stream-entry path without attaining any of the mundane jhanas.

FETTERS: The fetters are underlying tendencies in the mind that act as the roots of the hindrances. The fetters are the roots and the hindrances are their offshoots. The fetters arise directly from the contact of our senses with sensory objects and consciousness.

The fetters, in turn, grow in the base soil fed by the three poisons: greed, hatred, and delusion.

There are ten fetters. The first five are called lower, the last five higher. The ten fetters are belief in a permanent self; skeptical doubt; dependence upon rituals; craving for sensual pleasure; ill will; craving for a fine material existence; craving for an immaterial existence; conceit; restlessness; ignorance.

FIRST JHANA: Qualities of the first jhana include very little normal thought or sensation; subtle thoughts of good will and compassion; joy, happiness, equanimity, mindfulness, and concentration.

FOUR ELEMENTS: An analytical system to help you focus on the four foundations of mindfulness. The elements are *Earth* (solidity—the *Earth* element represents solidity, heaviness, solidness, compactness and is characterized by hardness or softness); *Water* (liquidity—the *Water* element has a moist or flowing quality); *Air* (oscillation—the *Air* element is experienced primarily as motion or stillness); *Fire* (heat; the *Fire* element manifests as heat or cold or any sense of temperature in between, or as the dry sensation that goes with heat).

FOUR FOUNDATIONS OF MINDFULNESS: See Satipatthana

FOURTH JHANA: Qualities of the fourth jhana include purified mindfulness and equanimity, mindfulness and concentration fused into a unit, direct perception of anicca, dukkha, and anatta.

HINDRANCES: Factors that hamper concentration. They get in your way and impede your progress along the path.

The Pali literature lists five things that are the most powerful distractions for all of us. We call them hindrances. They interfere with our concentration, on the cushion or off: sense desire; aversion; restlessness and worry; sloth and torpor; doubt.

In samadhi meditation we focus our minds on a certain object in order to suppress these hindrances and thus attain the mundane jhanas.

ILL WILL: When your motivation is unkind or aggressive, even a little, you have ill will. In that condition you cannot appreciate the beauty of anything or anybody. It is just like a man who is sick. He cannot enjoy any kind of delicious food because his taste buds are affected.

IMMATERIAL JHANAS: The immaterial jhanas are four states that have very little relationship to our ordinary cognitive/sensory world. These are called the "formless" jhanas. If numbered, they would be called the fifth, sixth, seventh, and eighth jhanas, but they are usually referred to with individual names.

IMPERMANENCE: See Anicca

JHANA: The jhanas are a sequence of mental states that become more and more insubstantial as we proceed through them. The word jhana derives from jha (from the Sanskrit *dyai*). It means to "burn," "suppress," or "absorb." "Jhana" is sometimes used to mean meditation in general, but usually the meaning is more specific.

Jhana means a deep, tranquil state of meditation, a balanced state of mind where numerous wholesome mental factors work together in harmony. In unison, they make the mind calm, relaxed, serene, peaceful, smooth, soft, pliable, bright, and equanimous. In that state of mind, mindfulness, effort, concentration, and understanding are consolidated. All these factors work together as a team.

Jhana is a term with two primary meanings. The first is the *Mundane Jhanas*, in which you focus your mind on a certain object and you suppress the hindrances to attain the fine material jhanas. You focus the mind on concepts to attain the immaterial jhanas. The second is *Supramundane Jhana*, in which you destroy psychic irritants (fetters) by seeing the characteristics of all objects through attaining supramundane jhana.

There are two categories of mundane jhana.

The first category does not have names. They are just numbered, simply called the first, second, third, and fourth jhanas. These are called the fine material jhanas. Those who have attained these jhanas are called "those who live happily in this very life."

The second category contains four refined states of consciousness. They do not have numbers, but names: the base of infinite space; the base of consciousness; the base of nothingness; the base of neither perception nor non-perception.

They are called immaterial jhanas because the meditation objects of these jhanas are pure concepts, not anything material. Those who have attained these jhanas are called "those who are liberated and live in peace."

Thus jhanas are divided into four subcategories:mundane jhanas (the jhanas pertaining to worldly attainments); the fine material or ruppa jhanas; the immaterial or aruppa jhanas; supramundane jhana (the jhana that stops repetition of birth and death).

The first three are ways of maintaining samsara. The last one is the means to stopping samsara.

Joy: The ordinary, material joy we are accustomed to arises from contacting things that are wished for. When you seek and know the impermanence, the change, the fading away, and the cessation of all these things, a different joy arises. This is called *joy based on renunciation.*

Kasina: A kasina is a physical object used as a meditation focus. Traditionally, they were circles used to represent certain concepts. Kasina means an object that represents a pure concept, the essence of all things with that quality.

Learning Sign: The object of focus itself is called a "preliminary sign" or "learning sign." The meditator gazes at it until he or she memorizes it. The memorized picture is called the "counterpart sign." The meditator holds this counterpart sign in mind and uses it as the meditation object to enter jhana.

Liberation: Termination of bondage; the state of being set free; Nibbana.

Light: See Luminosity

Luminosity: The mind is luminous. Jhana is where you see that clearly. The arising of the counterpart sign is often experienced as light. The mind is filled with a beautiful light. You see everything clearly.

Luminous: Referring to the bright and radiant nature of the basic mind.

Material Jhanas: The material jhanas are four states of experience that lie just beyond our ordinary cognitive, sensory world, but still have some relationship to it.

METTA: A state of mind characterized by loving-friendliness. One of the Four Brahmaviharas.

A meditation procedure in which you generate loving-friendliness toward yourself and all beings.

MINDFUL REFLECTION: A thought process that takes in what is happening at the moment, in the mind and body. It includes the deep nature of what you are experiencing, the effects that perception is having upon you, and the effects that it will have upon the mind in the future. It sometimes includes "talking to yourself."

MINDFULNESS: The quality of mind that notices and recognizes.

NEITHER PERCEPTION NOR NON-PERCEPTION: The "eighth jhana"— a state of awareness that is so subtle that it cannot be called perception or non-perception.

NEVER-RETURNER (NON-RETURNER): A stage of the supramundane path during which you eliminate the subtle remnants of hatred and greed for sensual pleasure.

NIBBANA: Literally "extinction." The highest and ultimate goal of Buddhist aspiration, absolute extinction of greed, hatred, delusion, and clinging to existence.

NOBLE EIGHTFOLD PATH: The eight steps of the Noble Eightfold Path must all be in place in your life in order to create the peaceful, settled atmosphere you need to cultivate jhanas.

The entire Noble Eightfold Path is divided into two parts—mundane and supramundane. The factors of the path can be either partially or fully developed.

NON-STICKINESS: A state in which nothing sticks to the mind. It all just flows through.

ONCE-RETURNER: The second stage of the supramundane path, during which you eliminate the gross parts of lust and hatred.

PALI: The ancient canonical language of Theravada Buddhism.

INFINITE SPACE: Perception of infinite space, the "fifth jhana"—a state of awareness in which the attention has been turned from an object of contemplation toward the mental "space" that the object formerly occupied.

INFINITE AWARENESS: Perception of infinite awareness, the "sixth jhana"—In the fifth jhana you dwelt upon the mental "space" within which experience takes place and expanded that to infinity. In the sixth jhana you dwell upon the infinite awareness that has that experience.

NOTHINGNESS: Perception of total voidness, the "seventh jhana"—In the sixth jhana you dwelt upon infinite awareness. In the seventh you turn the attention to the nothingness within that awareness.

PRELIMINARY SIGN: See Learning Sign

RESOLVING: Resolving is the ability to make a decision to remain in the jhana for exactly a predetermined length of time. You resolve or decide to spend a certain amount of time in jhana. This ability is weak in the lower jhanas and grows in the higher ones. This is part of jhana mastery.

RESTLESSNESS AND WORRY: One of the five hindrances. It is the opposite of sleepiness and drowsiness. You have "monkey mind." Your mind jumps about constantly. It refuses to settle down.

REVIEWING: This means the ability to review the jhana and its factors with retrospective knowledge immediately after adverting to them. You have noticed the factor; now you consciously review it. This is part of jhana mastery.

RIGHT CONCENTRATION: Right concentration (samma samadhi) is defined and explained in terms of five jhanas.

Mindfulness is the prerequisite and the basis of concentration. Mindfulness gradually increases as jhana practice is developed. It becomes pure in the fourth jhana due to the presence of equanimity. Mindfulness necessarily supports right concentration. Concentration without mindfulness is "wrong concentration."

RIGHT JHANA: See Right Concentration. Mindfulness is present in every state of "right jhana," along with the other seven factors of awakening.

RIGHT VERSUS WRONG CONCENTRATION: In the Noble Eightfold Path, concentration is qualified as "right" concentration in order to differentiate it from wrong concentration. There is no mindfulness in wrong concentration. You become attached to it. When you come out of wrong jhana, jhana that doesn't have mindfulness, you may think the experience you had was enlightenment.

SAMADHI: Jhana and samadhi are closely connected ideas but not the same thing. Jhana is limited in meaning; there must be five jhanic factors present. Samadhi means concentration in general. It derives from a prefixed verbal root that means to collect or to bring together. This suggests concentration or unification of mind. Samadhi can be either wholesome or unwholesome.

SAMAPATTI: The deepest stages of samadhi. In some Buddhist texts samadhi and samapatti are used synonymously.

SAMATHA: The word samatha, meaning "serenity," is almost inter-changeable with the word samadhi. Samatha, however, comes from a different root that means to become calm. Both are defined as "one-pointedness of mind." It is settling the emotional commotion of the mind, creating peace or composure. It can only be wholesome.

SAMPAJANNA: Clear comprehension, clarity of consciousness. Sam-pajanna means remaining fully awake and conscious in the midst of any activity, everything your body is doing and everything you are perceiving. It is a turned-within monitoring of everything going on in the mind and body.

SAMSARA: *Round of rebirth*—the continuous process of being reborn again and again, with suffering, illness, old age, and dying.

SATIPATTHANA: *Four Foundations of Mindfulness*—You can't get jhana through concentrating on just anything. You must use certain spe-cific subjects in your meditation. They must be things that promote dispassionate observation and reveal the truth of anicca, dukkha, and anatta: mindfulness of body (including breath); mindfulness of feel-ing (physical sensation); mindfulness of consciousness (thoughts);

mindfulness of dhammas (phenomena as mental activities, especially the primary ones, anicca, dukkha, and anatta).

SECLUSION: It is very important for the jhana practitioner to leave behind all work, all people, and all family concerns. In other words, all your normal worries and unease. This is physical separation and it is essential.

But physical separation is not enough. You need mental separation too. In this "liberation from attachment," you let go of your attachment to things, people, situations, and experiences too.

SECOND JHANA: Qualities of the second jhana include: subtle thought drops away; joy predominates; happiness, equanimity, mindfulness, and concentration are noticeably present.

SELFLESSNESS: See Anatta

SLOTH AND TORPOR: *Sloth and torpor* is the traditional description given to all sleepy, lethargic, sluggish states of mind. *Sleepiness and drowsiness* is another common translation.

STAGES OF THE SUPRAMUNDANE PATH: There are said to be stages in the enlightenment process. They are stream entry; once-returner; never-returner; arahant.

They occur in that order. Each stage is marked by the lessening or elimination of one or more of the fetters. The order in which these are destroyed depends upon your personality type. Faith-followers destroy the fetters in one order. Dhamma-followers proceed by another sequence. Each stage consists of a "path" and a "fruition" phase.

STREAM ENTRY: A stage of the supramundane path. This is the moment that you really see the Dhamma. You eliminate doubt, dependence on rituals, and the notion of self.

SUFFERING: See Dukkha

SUPRAMUNDANE JHANA: The states of jhanic consciousness that the noble ones have in the phases of enlightenment called stream entry, once-returner, never-returner, and arahant.

Complete burning of the fetters leading to escape from samsara.

Supramundane unification of mind is a noble, stainless state that abolishes any unwholesome mental condition. It is written that, if the meditator attains supramundane jhana without attaining full enlightenment, he will be reborn a limited number of times, and only in higher planes of existence. Attaining full enlightenment brings rebirth to an end completely.

THE PATH: The Noble Eightfold Path.

THIRD JHANA: Qualities of the third jhana include: joy drops away; happiness predominates; equanimity, mindfulness, and concentration grow.

THIRTY-SEVEN FACTORS OF ENLIGHTENMENT: Liberation is said to have components. A "factor" is a feature or aspect of something. It is a dynamic thing, often a cause of something else, often something you must do or have in order to make that second thing come into existence. In this case, a factor is something that must be present in order for enlightenment to take place.

There are thirty-seven factors of enlightenment and they are divided into seven overlapping groups: the seven factors of awakening; the Noble Eightfold Path; the four foundations of mindfulness; the four efforts; the four bases for spiritual power; the five spiritual faculties; the five spiritual powers.

UNMINDFUL REFLECTION: A thought process that does not notice what is happening at the moment, in the mind and body. It is a state of being totally immersed in a thought process without mindfulness of its nature. It neglects to observe the deep nature of what you are experiencing, the effects that thought is having upon you, and the effects that it will have upon the mind in the future.

UNSATISFACTORINESS: See Dukkha

VIPASSANA: *Insight*—This is the intuitive perception and understanding of anicca, dukkha, and anatta.

VITAKKA / VICARA: Vitakka is called "thought" or "thought conception." It is the laying hold of a thought. It is likened to the striking of a bell.

Vicara is called "discursive thought." It is the mind roaming about or moving back and forth over thoughts. It is likened to the reverberation or resounding of the bell.

Vitakka and vicara are present in normal consciousness and in the first jhana, but absent in every jhana above the first.

VOIDNESS: Things flow through the mind. They leave no trace. You see void or vacuum in what has been lost. The word may also refer to the immaterial jhana called perception of nothingness.

WISDOM-FOLLOWER: Someone whose primary vehicle on the path is wisdom. He uses the intellect extensively. His primary vehicle is a deep understanding of the Dhamma. His reason leads him to the deep, wordless understanding that is true wisdom. A wisdom-follower can attain stream entry through penetrative insight alone, without attaining jhana.

WRONG CONCENTRATION: Wrong concentration is absorption concentration without the other seven factors of the Noble Eightfold Path. Without them, vipassana is not successful. Because you have not developed jhana with mindfulness, you become attached to the jhanic state. How do you know your concentration is wrong concentration? One clue is absence of all feeling. You will not have any feeling only when you have attained the highest jhana known as the attainment of "cessation of perception and feelings." Until such time you certainly have feelings and perceptions.

WRONG JHANA: Jhana without mindfulness; see Wrong Concentration.

Further and Recommended Reading

Breath by Breath: The Liberating Practice of Insight Meditation
by Larry Rosenberg

Eight Mindful Steps to Happiness: Walking the Buddha's Path
by Bhante Henepola Gunaratana

*Focused and Fearless: A Meditator's Guide to States
of Deep Joy, Calm and Clarity*
by Shaila Catherine

Food for the Heart: The Collected Teachings of Ajahn Chah
by Ajahn Chah

Insight Meditation: The Practice of Freedom
by Joseph Goldstein

*In the Buddha's Words: An Anthology of Discourses
from the Pali Canon*
edited by Bhikkhu Bodhi

Lovingkindness: The Revolutionary Art of Happiness
    by Sharon Salzberg

Meditation for Beginners
    by Jack Kornfield

Mindfulness in Plain English
    by Bhante Henepola Gunaratana

Mindfulness, Bliss, and Beyond: A Meditator's Handbook
    by Ajahn Brahm

*The Attention Revolution: Unlocking the Power
    of the Focused Mind*
    by B. Alan Wallace

The Beginner's Guide to Insight Meditation
    by Arinna Weisman and Jean Smith

The Meditator's Atlas: A Roadmap to the Inner World
    by Matthew Flickstein

Index

About the Author

VENERABLE HENEPOLA GUNARATANA was ordained at the age of twelve as a Buddhist monk in Malandeniya, Sri Lanka. In 1947, at age twenty, he was given higher ordination in Kandy. He received his education from Vidyasekhara Junior College in Gumpaha, Vidyalankara College in Kelaniya, and Buddhist Missionary College in Colombo. Subsequently he traveled to India for five years of missionary work for the Mahabodhi Society, serving the Harijana ("untouchable") people in Sanchi, Delhi, and Bombay. Later he spent ten years as a missionary in Malaysia, serving as religious advisor to the Sasana Abhivurdhiwardhana Society, the Buddhist Missionary Society, and the Buddhist Youth Federation of Malaysia. He has been a teacher in Kishon Dial School and Temple Road Girls' School and principal of the Buddhist Institute of Kuala Lumpur.

At the invitation of the Sasana Sevaka Society, he came to the United States in 1968 to serve as general secretary of the Buddhist Vihara Society of Washington, D.C. In 1980, he was appointed president of the society. During his years at the Vihara, from 1968 to 1988, he taught courses in Buddhism, conducted meditation retreats, and lectured widely throughout the United States, Canada, Europe, Australia, New Zealand, Africa, and Asia. In addition, from 1973 to 1988, Venerable Gunaratana served as Buddhist chaplain at American University.

He has also pursued his scholarly interests by earning a Ph.D. in philosophy from American University. He has taught courses on Buddhism at American University, Georgetown University, and the University of Maryland. His books and articles have been published in Malaysia, India, Sri Lanka, and the United States. *Mindfulness in Plain English* has been translated into many languages and published around the world. An abridged Thai translation has been selected for use in the high school curriculum throughout Thailand.

Since 1982 Venerable Gunaratana has been president of the Bhavana Society, a monastery and retreat center located in the woods of West Virginia (near the Shenandoah Valley), which he cofounded with Matthew Flickstein. Venerable Gunaratana resides at the Bhavana Society, where he ordains and trains monks and nuns, and offers retreats to the general public. He also travels frequently to lecture and lead retreats throughout the world.

In 2000, Venerable Gunaratana received an award for lifetime outstanding achievement from his alma mater, Vidyalankara College.

More Books by Bhante Gunaratana from Wisdom Publications

EIGHT MINDFUL STEPS TO HAPPINESS
Walking the Buddha's Path

"Written with the thoroughness and the masterful simplicity so characteristic of his teaching, Bhante Gunaratana presents essential guidelines for turning the Buddha's teachings on the eightfold path into living wisdom."—Larry Rosenberg, author of *Breath By Breath*

JOURNEY TO MINDFULNESS
The Autobiography of Bhante G.

"Like the stories of the wisest and kindest of grandfathers. A joy to read."— Sylvia Boorstein, author of *It's Easier Than You Think*

MINDFULNESS IN PLAIN ENGLISH
20th-Anniversary Edition

"A masterpiece. I cannot recommend it highly enough."—Jon Kabat-Zinn, author of *Wherever You Go, There You Are*

FOUR FOUNDATIONS OF MINDFULNESS IN PLAIN ENGLISH

"Bhante Gunaratana's works stand out for their depth of wisdom, clarity of expression, and warm-hearted accessibility. *The Four Foundations of Mindfulness in Plain English* continues this tradition of exceptionally helpful dharma teachings."—Joseph Goldstein, author of *A Heart Full of Peace*

MEDITATION ON PERCEPTION
Ten Healing Practices to Cultivate Mindfulness

"Clear and concise, this book is invaluable."—Toni Bernhard, author of *How to Live Well with Chronic Pain and Illness*

START HERE, START NOW
A Short Guide to Mindfulness Meditation

"A timeless, clear, and beautiful introduction."—Tamara Levitt, Head of Mindfuless at Calm

WHAT, WHY, HOW
Answers to Your Questions About Buddhism, Meditation, and Living Mindfully

"This book can be of help to anyone's spiritual journey and meditation practice."—Sharon Salzberg, author of *Lovingkindness and Real Happiness*

Also Available from Wisdom Publications

WISDOM WIDE AND DEEP
A Practical Handbook for Mastering Jhana and Vipassana
Shaila Catherine

"If you are interested in Dharma study, then Shaila's book belongs in your library."—Phillip Moffitt

FOCUSED AND FEARLESS
A Meditator's Guide to States of Deep Joy, Calm, and Clarity
Shaila Catherine

"A beautifully written introduction to jhana meditation that demonstrates the importance and necessity of deep concentration."
—Venerable Pa-Auk Tawya Sayadaw

MINDFULNESS, BLISS, AND BEYOND
A Meditator's Handbook
Ajahn Brahm
Foreword by Jack Kornfield

"A masterpiece. I cannot recommend it highly enough."—Jon Kabat-Zinn, author of *Wherever You Go, There You Are*

DON'T WORRY, BE GRUMPY
Inspiring Stories for Making the Most of Each Moment
Ajahn Brahm

"If a picture is worth a thousand words, then a good metaphorical story is worth that many more. Ajahn Brahm's latest collection of stories is funny, endearing, and, of course, infused with wisdom."
—Arnie Kozak, author of *Mindfulness A to Z*

THE ART OF DISAPPEARING
The Buddha's Path to Lasting Joy
Ajahn Brahm

"In this illuminating work, Brahm shines a light on the spiritual practice of mindfulness."—*Spirituality & Practice*

WHO ORDERED THIS TRUCKLOAD OF DUNG?
Inspiring Stories for Welcoming Life's Difficulties
Ajahn Brahm

"Ajahn Brahm is the Seinfeld of Buddhism."—Sumi Loundon Kim, editor of *Blue Jean Buddha*

MANUAL OF INSIGHT
Mahasi Sayadaw
Foreword by Joseph Goldstein and Daniel Goleman

"The teachings of Mahasi Sayadaw formed the essential context in which I learned, practiced, and studied meditation. That context is beautifully expressed in this book."—Sharon Salzberg, author of *Lovingkindness*

About Wisdom Publications

Wisdom Publications is the leading publisher of classic and contemporary Buddhist books and practical works on mindfulness. To learn more about us or to explore our other books, please visit our website at wisdomexperience.org or contact us at the address below.

Wisdom Publications
199 Elm Street
Somerville, MA 02144 USA

We are a 501(c)(3) organization, and donations in support of our mission are tax deductible.

Wisdom Publications is affiliated with the Foundation for the Preservation of the Mahayana Tradition (FPMT).